Her Space,  Story

Her Space, Her Story

Exploring the Stepwells of Gujarat

PURNIMA MEHTA BHATT

Photographs by
DANIEL DEL SOLAR

zubaan

ZUBAAN
an imprint of Kali for Women
128 B Shahpur Jat, 1st floor
NEW DELHI 110 049
Email: contact@zubaanbooks.com
Website: www.zubaanbooks.com

First published by Zubaan 2014

Copyright © Purnima Mehta Bhatt

10 9 8 7 6 5 4 3 2 1

ISBN 978 93 83074 49 5

Zubaan is an independent feminist publishing house based in New Delhi with a strong academic and general list. It was set up as an imprint of India's first feminist publishing house, Kali for Women, and carries forward Kali's tradition of publishing world quality books to high editorial and production standards. *Zubaan* means tongue, voice, language, speech in Hindustani. Zubaan is a non-profit publisher, working in the areas of the humanities, social sciences, as well as in fiction, general non-fiction, and books for children and young adults under its Young Zubaan imprint.

Typeset by Jojy Phillip, New Delhi 110 015
Printed at Raj Press, R-3 Inderpuri, New Delhi 110 012

For Kiran and Daniel

'Fortunate, indeed, is he who has but once seen a stepwell;
success in all his works follows him'

Anonymous

Contents

List of Photographs   ix

Acknowledgements   xi

1   Introduction   1

2   Significance and Sanctity of Water in India   5

3   Origin and Development of Stepwells (7th–19th Centuries) 14

4   The Woman Factor   24

5   Description of Individual Stepwells   35

6   Place of Women in Society   60

7   Queen's Stepwell (Rani ni vav) – Patan, Gujarat   72

8   Voices from the Deep   91

9   Art, Symbolism and the Iconography of Stepwells   107

10 Birds and Nature in the Stepwells of Gujarat   120

11 Stepwells Today   133

Bibliography   140

About the Author and Photographer   147

Index   149

List of Photographs

5.1 Women descending the steps to the water at Adalaj   49
5.2 A view of Adalaj landing platforms and pillars   50
5.3 View of the ornately decorated walls at Adalaj   50
5.4 Dada Harir stepwell showing water channels   52
7.1 Queen's stepwell—A view from the top   74
7.2 A view of the Patan stepwell wall   75
7.3 Sculptures adorning the Queen's stepwell, Patan   76
7.4 Maiden applying lipstick   76
7.5 A panel from the Queen's stepwell   77
7.6 Maiden with a monkey climbing up her left leg   77
7.7 Lattice pattern on the stepwell walls   78
7.8 Maiden with a scorpion climbing up her right leg   79
7.9 A woman with an infant   88
7.10 Queen's stepwell, Patan   90
9.1 Mahishasura Mardini slaying the buffalo-headed demon 109
9.2 Varaha with the Earth Goddess   112
9.3 Elephants and lion at play   117
10.1 Maiden with a parrot   130

10.2 Maiden and the swan   131
11.1 Mother Goddess riding a rooster   134
11.2 Local Goddess riding a tiger   135
11.3 Modern day shrine of Devi   135
11.4 Discarded ritual clay pots   136
11.5 Mata Bhavani temple   137

Acknowledgements

Many individuals provided me immense help during the course of my research. I would like to express my appreciation to them for without their support, encouragement and assistance, this book would not have been published. I would especially like to thank Daniel del Solar for his unbounded enthusiasm during our trips to photograph the stepwells and Dr Ramjibhai Savalia, Director of B. J. Institute, Ahmedabad for his continuous support. I also would like to thank Ms Rafikaben Sultana, Curator of the Museum at Gujarat Vidyapith, and Dr Kansara and Ms Sudha Mehta for help in translating the Gujarati folk songs and poems. This project was made possible through a sabbatical leave from Hood College. Most of all, I am indebted to Kiran, Anuradha and my mother, who shared my excitement about this project every step of the way.

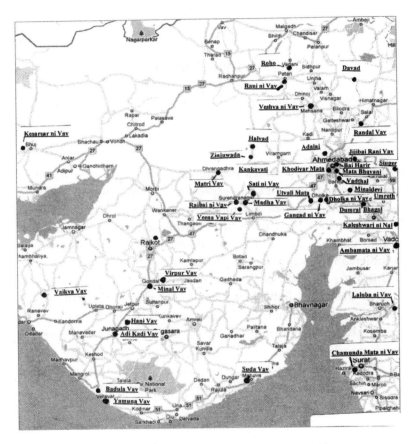

Important stepwells in Gujarat which were commissioned by women or built to honour them

Women with water pots on their way to the wells (Photograph courtesy of Kingdom of Grace Ministries)

1

Introduction

This book examines and documents the role women played in the building and patronage of and as inspiration for the numerous stepwells of Gujarat from the seventh to the nineteenth centuries. It provides a historical analysis and visual documentation of the stepwells, thereby contributing to a better understanding of the relationship between women, water, architecture and religion. My book has a unique perspective: it examines the stepwells primarily as a distinct space for women.

In the past decade, a number of excellent and carefully researched books on stepwells have been published, notably Morna Livingston's *Steps to Water: The Ancient Stepwells of India*; Jutta Jain-Neubauer's *The Stepwells of Gujarat: In Art–Historical Perspective*; Kirit Mankodi's *The Queen's Stepwell at Patan*; and Jaikishandas Sadani's *The Underground Shrine: Queen's Stepwell at Patan*, along with numerous monographs and articles. These scholarly works have made a major contribution to enhancing our knowledge of the stepwells, and I owe a debt of gratitude to them. However, this book will be the first to focus on the unique perspective of 'the woman factor'. More often than not, women appear as silent spectators in history, not active participants. Recent scholarship points to an urgent need to call into question why women's lives, their contributions and perspectives have been so vastly neglected. There is a compelling urgency, I believe, to correct the historical record to more accurately reflect women's perspectives and achievements, to hear their voices, which have remained silent for so many centuries, and to make the invisible, visible.

I first encountered stepwells nearly half a century ago when, on a summer vacation, I visited my grandparents in Ahmedabad, Gujarat. My grandmother arranged for me to join a day long sightseeing tour of the architectural marvels and historical sights in and around Ahmedabad. It was during the course of this trip that I first visited the stepwell of Adalaj and was struck by its unique grandeur and artistic beauty.

Many decades later, I learned that these stepwells, which are a familiar feature of the landscape of Gujarat, once numbered in the thousands. In the dry, arid and parched land where water is scarce and the rains are scanty, these wells provided life-giving water to humans and animals, and enabled the land to become fertile and crops to flourish. What was even more intriguing was that of the several hundred stepwells that have been excavated, around 25 per cent were actually built by women—queens, royalty, wives of rich merchants, ordinary women, courtesans and servant girls—who hoped to gain religious merit and possibly immortality through the gift of water.

Not only did women commission many of the stepwells as patrons and donors, they also frequently served as the inspiration—stepwells were built to honour and were named after a virtuous wife or a benevolent mother, a local goddess or a beloved mistress. As new research is undertaken with a greater sensitivity to gender issues, it is exciting to envision that more women will emerge as patrons of art and architecture. 'Women's agency' in art will receive the attention it merits.

And it was women who used the stepwells to fetch water for daily use. The stepwells were viewed as 'women's space', where women came not only to fill their brass pots with water, but also to linger awhile to talk and gossip, share their joys and sorrows, and seek the solace and companionship of other women.

Women gathered at these stepwells to obtain water but also to appeal to the local deities for health, happiness and children. They performed rituals to ensure their own fertility, to ask for the gift of sons, to ask the goddess to intercede on their behalf so that milk would flow from their breasts to nurture their newborn. These age-old rituals in and around the stepwells continue even today. As a gathering place for women where they came to fetch water, the stepwells became a favorite subject in folklore. Every step of these stepwells yields tales of love and betrayal, courage and sacrifice. I have attempted to identify and translate some of these songs and tales that tell us about the inner lives of the women whose voices still echo in these now crumbling and dilapidated structures.

These stepwells are unique structures because they were not merely utilitarian buildings; they served a dual function—providing water but also as a site for ritual and propitiation of the local deities. They linked three worlds: the subterranean, the earthly, and the celestial.

All kinds of questions arose in my mind. For example, if stepwells can be viewed as 'women's space', would it not then follow that the art and images that embellish these structures reflect the religious and aesthetic stirrings of these women? If stepwells became, over time, the focal point of women's rituals, would they not reveal to us more about women's religious beliefs and daily rituals? Since women were the patrons and donors of many of these stepwells, did they influence or shape the thematic choices of the images carved on the walls and pillars? Did this art represent a different reality? Is there any basis to suggest that unlike the sculptures in Hindu temples, which celebrate the male deities—Vishnu, Shiva and Brahma, the deities who appear most frequently in the stepwells are the '*devis*', the local goddesses?[1]

According to my research, the art of the stepwells looks beyond the patriarchal gods of classical Hinduism and instead honours and celebrates the feminine principle, the creative force in the Universe. The goddess in her manifested forms is visible everywhere in the

[1] The term '*devi*' refers to a goddess, a female deity. She is worshipped as Amba, Chamunda, Shikkotari, Lakshmi, Parvati, Sitala or by many other names.

stepwells, occupying not the servile position of the Brahmin wife, but a place of pre-eminence. Were these wells an indication of women's growing power and wealth in society, their striving to place themselves in history's gaze and thereby challenging the stereotypes of their passivity? Do these stepwells provide a unique and different perspective on women? Did women's patronage affect the artistic and aesthetic aspects of these structures?

I hope this book, despite its limitations, will serve as a catalyst for further research and encourage scholars and the 'merely curious' to explore in much greater depth the lives and contributions of women in all spheres of activity. There is much we can learn by giving a voice to the countless women forgotten and neglected by history. In doing so, we will have succeeded in some measure in 'making the invisible, visible'.

2

Significance and Sanctity of Water in India

It goes without saying that water is essential for survival; from the very beginnings of human culture it played a vital role in the abundance of crops, prosperity in agriculture, and the birth and flowering of civilisations. In Sanskrit, one meaning of the word '*jeevan*' (life) is 'water'. In other words, water equates life itself. Water is referred to as '*Jeevanam Sarva Jeevanam*' meaning that the entire world depends on water for survival (quoted in Savalia, 2000, p. 94). Water is an essential ingredient in rituals and ceremonies in all religious traditions of the world—this is especially true in India where it plays a vital role in funerals, births and marriages.

In Gujarat, a hot tropical region that is also dry and arid, water can make the difference between life and death. Since rainfall is scarce, except during the monsoons, and most rivers are devoid of water during the dry season, the inhabitants of the region devised different ways to obtain, store and manage water—these included rivers, ponds, lakes, wells and stepwells.

In a parched land, the gift of water was precious and quenching the thirst of humans and beasts was viewed as meritorious—an act that gained great merit for the giver. Consequently, men and women of means—kings and queens, wealthy merchants, traders and occasionally even common folk—provided funds and patronised the construction of wells and stepwells. Such acts of charity gained them merit as well as the promise of '*moksha*' or immortality.

PURIFICATORY AND CURATIVE POWERS OF WATER

Literary references and archaeological evidence of the purificatory powers of water are available from the beginning of Indian culture. Excavations carried out in 1922 on the banks of the river Indus unearthed the Indus Valley Civilisation dating back 4,500 years ago. Those excavations revealed the existence of large public baths as well as individual bathing spaces in the multi-storeyed homes of the rich, providing clear evidence of the importance of water for purification and as an integral aspect of religious ritual and worship. The religious significance of water continues throughout Indian history, right up to the present, evident in the use of the sacred waters in ceremonies relating to the rites of passage—birth, initiation, marriage and death.

Numerous hymns and verses in the Rig Veda, the earliest religious and literary text dating back to 1500 BCE, contain elements of water worship and praise for the apsaras, who represent the anthropomorphic form of water. The apsaras, or celestial nymphs, are described as mothers or young wives who reside in the channels leading up to the sea (Keith, 1925, pp. 141–42). Water was also worshipped in the form of the god Varuna. People believed that the ancestral spirits resided in the waters and could be invoked in places such as water buildings.

In the Vedic tradition, water is said to be endowed with transformative and magical powers (Rig Veda I.23; 17–22). Referring to the healing qualities of waters, the Rig Veda (I.23; 19–20) states:

> *Amrta is in the waters; in the*
> *waters, there is healing balm; Be swift,*
> *ye Gods, to give them praise.*
> *Within the waters — the waters hold all medicines.*

The other ancient texts, the Puranas, provide elaborate descriptions of water worship. From these we know that wells, ponds and tanks became associated with sacred altars, the site for rituals and worship. The belief that water bestows long life, wealth and immortality are clearly evident in these texts, along with the belief that they cleanse the sins of the worshiper. In Matsya Purana, there are numerous descriptions of water buildings—such as ponds, lakes and wells; these became pilgrimage sites. The Vamana Purana describing the Manas Sarovar says that he who bathes in its waters will gain paradise and enjoy the company of apsaras. It is stated in the Padma Purana that whoever builds water buildings will enjoy thousands of years of paradise. The same text goes on to say that those who bathe in its waters and worship it will gain much wealth. Bathing in the waters obtained from certain wells was believed to have the power to expiate sins, similar to the efficacy of a dip in the sacred waters of the river Ganges. The Agni Purana states that one who consecrates wells, tanks and ponds 'can never get any sin as the cattle and other (animals) drink water from it. One attains all merits by the endowment of water and goes to heaven' (Agni Purana, 64. 30–40, p. 178). Certain water structures are associated with mythological figures. Ayodhya Mahatmya contains an appreciation of Sita *kund* (pond), which is believed to have been built by Sita herself (the heroine of the epic Ramayana, a beloved figure in Hindu mythology who is the embodiment of wifely devotion and feminine virtues), while the waters of Rukmini *kund* (Rukmini was Krishna's wife) are said to fulfill all human desires (Savalia, 2011). The waters of the stepwells and wells, though stagnant, are regarded as both pure and clean. This is because of the prevailing belief that the sun is the great purifier of water, and water structures like wells, stepwells and ponds were rarely closed or covered.

Many different legends relating to the magical powers residing in water became popular. There is a stepwell (called a 'vav' in Gujarati) on Mount Girnar in Saurashtra known as Raskupika vav. It is said that the body of a person who falls in its waters becomes hard as marble and a coin or stone, if dipped into the waters, is transformed into gold (Enthoven, 1914, p. 38). However, the vav is only visible to holy men and sages who possess mystical and supernatural powers.

Another stepwell in Varanasi called Kashipuri or Jnana vav is said to contain an image of Vishveshwar, the lord of the universe. According to this legend, whoever bathes in these waters acquires the gift of divine knowledge. There are numerous other references to sacred ponds and wells. Yogini *kund's* waters are said to be the abode of 64 female ascetics who fulfill all the desires of humans. Women who bathe in the Sukanya pond will enjoy domestic bliss and health and wealth for their husbands for 7,000 births (Savalia, 2000, p. 12).

The waters of certain stepwells were regarded as especially sacred and beneficial. The cool and sweet water of the Selor stepwell in Kutch was said to have greater sanctity than visiting a temple. Annual fairs and festivals were held here on certain days of the year (Pathak, 1997, p. 170). Other stepwells were believed to possess unique and magical qualities. An example of this is the Vajeriyani vav in Tilakwada district, the waters of which are believed to sharpen the blades of metal tools.

Stepwells are also often seen as the abode of local goddesses or ghosts and spirits. The goddess Rainadevi is said to reside in the waters and is worshipped by young unmarried maidens on the 15th day of the month of *Asadh* (Enthoven and Jackson, 1989, p. 40). On this day, they offer the goddess newly sprouted wheat plants (*javaras*) in earthen vessels with the hope of attaining husbands and fertility. These represent the living tradition in Gujarat.

Stories of ghosts haunting vavs are numerous. According to popular lore, a *pinjari* (female cotton carder) is said to have drowned in a vav called Nilkantha near Movaiya. She subsequently turned into a ghost and appears in this form at the vav. Another story is associated with an old stepwell called Madha in Wadhwan where one human is said to drown every third year (ibid., p. 38).

There is a prevailing belief among the people that mischievous and malevolent spirits haunt the wayside wells and drown or possess those who go near the wells. Known as *jalachar* (living in the water), these are said to be restless spirits of persons who died in accidents or by drowning and must be placated to prevent harm (Masani, 1978, p. 76). Water spirits are generally believed to be beneficent but there also exist the mischievous and malevolent spirits, which could cause harm, and therefore need to be appeased and placated.

WATER AND FERTILITY

The association of water with fertility dates back to antiquity. Water was seen as the symbol of fertility, not merely of the land and cattle but of humans too. Bathing in the sacred water of rivers, lakes, ponds and wells was thus prescribed as a cure for barrenness. Women who wanted a son or who were barren would bathe in the sacred water that they believed had mystical powers. In Dhanduka district's Aakrun village, there is a 250-year-old stepwell with a shrine to the local mother goddess; a similar stepwell exists in Dadva village in Saurashtra whose powers enable women to bear children. Many water structures such as wells were thus transformed into shrines where women came to perform rites and rituals for fertility. The sacred yellow turmeric powder sprinkled on the images of the deities found in the niches on the walls suggests ripe grain; milk is symbolic of mother's milk. Women who had difficulty in nursing are said to bathe in the Than vav and other stepwells which are believed to possess magical qualities to produce milk from the breasts of the mothers. In the Sabarkantha district of Gujarat, there is a pond known as Balasamudra *kund*. In popular folklore, there exists a belief that a woman who is unable to produce breast milk after the birth of her child should visit this *kund*; her blouse or *choli* is dipped in its waters after which, when she wears the blouse, the magical qualities of the water will enable her to nurse her new born.

It was also a commonly held belief that *apsara*s or the celestial nymphs along with the *gandharva*s or the divine musicians preside over fertility. The *apsara*s are perceived as young mothers and said to reside in rivers, clouds and the stars. According to Satpatha Brahmana, they possess the powers of metamorphosis and can transform themselves into aquatic birds (Keith, 1925, pp. 94–95). It is, therefore, not surprising that *apsara*s and *gandharva*s are depicted prolifically in stepwell art.

HEALING POWERS OF WATER

Wells were also said to be invested with supernatural powers, their water seen as the dwelling place for spirits. The water contained medicinal properties to heal the sick and cure the afflicted. These spirits, when invoked, could protect and guard against harm.

The ancient texts describe the healing powers of water said to cure all types of disease and ailments. One such passage in the Rig Veda states:

> *Healing are the watery billows,*
> *Water cools the fever's glow.*
> *Healing against every plague,*
> *Health to thee brings water's flow*
> — (Quoted in Kumar, 1983, p. 6).

An example of the curative power of water is the popular belief that anyone with an earache who made offerings of *ghee* in the stepwell known as Malanvar in Kutch would be cured of the pain. Consequently, *ghee* stains can be found all the way down to the water and those seeking a cure light lamps and make offerings. Another example comes from the city of Pātan. According to popular lore, many years ago, the residents of this city utilised the waters of the stepwell of Patan to treat a variety of ailments such as cough and whooping cough. They drilled tiny holes in the stones found scattered around the stepwell and tied them around the neck of the children for protection and made offerings of *ghee* lamps to propitiate the spirits (Valand, 2000, p. 21). Similarly, the wells near Ramdorana and the Bahmania well near Vasawad are credited with curing coughs, while the Pipli well near Talawad is known to alleviate digestive problems (Masani, 1918, p. 55). The waters of some wells and stepwells were believed to cure a variety of ailments – from cough to skin diseases (See Chapter 8 on folklore).

It is evident that the healing and curative powers residing in the waters of the wells caused them to be venerated. Various types of offerings were made at the wells which include sweets, sugar, honey, betel nuts, flowers, milk and coconuts. As sacred sites, the wells were covered with *jalis* or trellis work and illuminated with ghee lamps. It is a common practice all over India to install *dhajas* or flags near temples, religious buildings, shrines, pilgrimage sites and sacred trees. This was also the case with certain wells and stepwells which were said to be the abode of deities or spirits (ibid., pp. 104–05).

CONSTRUCTION OF WELLS AND INAUGURAL CEREMONIES

Sanskrit texts like Agni Purana,[1] Shilpa Shastra and others provide detailed guidelines and instructions relating to the construction and opening of wells.

Prior to the construction of a new well, an expert was recruited to select a favourable site. These experts or water diviners are said to possess unique powers of being able to hear the sound of running water underground. For others, an appropriate site is revealed through dreams. These water diviners or *panikals* are known as 'Bhonyesunghna' in Gujarat and Kutch, and as 'Sunga' in Punjab. Their judgement was said to be unerring. They could predict with accuracy the depth at which the water could be tapped (Masani, 1918, pp. 104–105.)

Ceremonies Marking the Digging of the Well

There are detailed accounts of ceremonies marking the digging and opening of the well. These involved the selection of an auspicious hour by the priest who, accompanied by the water diviner, the constructor of the well and the labourers,[2] would visit the proposed site to propitiate the deities. According to popular lore, Tuesdays and other days on which the earth sleeps must be avoided as also the first,

---

[1] The Agni Purana provides a detailed description of the mode of consecration of wells and the necessary rituals to be performed on this occasion (Agni Puranam, 1967, Chapter 64).

[2] In Gujarat and Rajasthan, the construction of the wells and stepwells was carried out by the caste of craftsmen or labourers known as 'Somparas'.

seventh, ninth, tenth, fourteenth and twenty-fourth days following Sankranti and the day when the sun crosses from one constellation to another.

On the appointed day, the image of the god Ganapati (Ganesh) is installed while the priest recites sacred hymns and offers *panchamrit*—a mixture of milk, curds, honey, sugar and coconuts— to Ganapati and the goddess Jaladevi. A green silk cloth is spread out on the spot and wheat, betel nuts, copper coins are placed on it. According to Masani, a copper bowl filled with water and gold/ silver coins are also placed, and the mouth of the bowl is covered with mango leaves on which is placed a coconut. This ceremony is known as the 'Khat-puja' (Masani, 1918, p. 106). This ceremony prescribed by the *shastra*s is intended to propitiate the mother Earth and to prevent interruptions. The ancient text of Aparajitaprccha provides a description of the deities to be installed in the stepwells and ponds. Visva Karma Vastusastra states that images of gods and ornamentation in the form of *Kinnara*[3] are to be made in the stepwell. Images of Varuna, the god of the waters, and other gods should be placed in a water monument. Varuna is depicted riding on a sea monster or *makara*.

Other sculptural images in the wells include that of Kshetrapala, the guardian of the location; *Navagraha* or the nine planets; Lakulisha, the last incarnation of Lord Shiva; Sitala, the goddess of smallpox; Surasundari also known as Rambha, symbolizing celestial beauty which emerged from the churning of the cosmic ocean;[4] and the *gandharva*s or celestial musicians. According to Enthoven and Jackson, the image of the deity Ganapati is buried underground and a brick laid on it prior to the commencement of the construction of the well (1989, p. 38).

---

[3] *Kinnara* is a heavenly being depicted as half man and half bird.
[4] Lakulisha is said to be the twenty-eighth incarnation of Lord Shiva and believed to be the founder of the Pashupata Sect of S'aivism. Sitala, the goddess of small pox, is worshipped all over India and depicted as a young woman with a winnowing fan riding an ass. She holds a broom in her hand and a jar of water in the other. Surasundari is a divine nymph whose image is found in temples and stepwell art.

Wells, thus, are sacred spaces, and are venerated by offerings of flowers, milk, sweets, coconuts and betel nuts. The niches in the walls are illuminated with oil lamps, intended to scare away evil spirits and the walls smeared with red lac. Often times one can also see flags (*dhajas*) hoisted near sacred wells or in nearby trees to frighten away the spirits.

3

Origin and Development of Stepwells (7th–19th Centuries)

BACKGROUND

Gujarat in western India has been dry and arid from time immemorial. Except during the summer, when torrential rains fall between June and August, the northern and western parts of Gujarat are like a desert. In response to the chronic water shortages, the inhabitants of this region developed strategies for harvesting, storing and preserving the water from the annual monsoons. For this purpose, wells, stepwells and other water structures were built from the 7th uptil the 19th century. Stepwells known as vav or vapika differed from ordinary wells because they had steps leading down to the water and did not require ropes to draw the water. They were also often more elaborate multi-storied structures embellished with art and sculpture.

These structures became a familiar feature of the landscape of western India. The stepwells were a source of life giving water which enabled the land to become fertile and the crops to flourish. The stepwells primarily served a utilitarian function. They also served a vital function as a gathering place for women who came here for water, solace, gossip and exchange of ideas and information, and sites for architectural and sculptural beauty and embellishment.

The region of Gujarat was a vital link in the trade between the north and south. It was located at the crossroads of trade routes. From time immemorial, caravans laden with cotton textiles, silk, indigo dye, pearls, carpets and other goods travelled through this region carrying precious cargo bound for distant lands. In the old days, merchants known as 'Vanjaras' travelled long distances with their merchandise and trade goods loaded on their bullock carts and camels. These traders and merchants often travelled at night guided by the stars and tried to avoid the fierce midday sun. The stepwells, thus, provided not just water for them and their animals but also a dark, cool place, where they could avoid the scorching sun and rejuvenate themselves surrounded by the images of gods and goddesses, and plants and animals on the decorated pillars and walls. In the absence of rest houses and caravanserais, the stepwells offered a place to rest.

Many stepwells therefore were built along ancient highways and in the vicinity of small villages and towns that lacked rivers, ponds and lakes and other easily accessible sources of water. Thus they were invaluable. Stepwells were built by rich merchants and, in the absence of the identity of the donor, were referred to as 'Vanjara ni vav' or the merchant's well.

Women, pilgrims, itinerant traders, troops on the march and royal hunting parties used these stepwells for water and rest. The landing platforms and ornamental galleries decorated with figurative carvings of deities, animal and plant motifs served as an escape and distraction from their monotonous journeys. They spent a few hours here in these underground buildings to eat their meals, drink the cool water and enjoy a few hours of rest and recuperation. The labyrinthine interior of the stepwell and the dark, cool environment enabled them to revive their spirit and rejuvenate the soul. Charles Moore has aptly stated that 'still waters evoke mystery.' Thus, stepwells represent the contemplative and pervasive 'indwelling spirit of nature' (Moore, 1994, p. 122). These stepwells therefore provided shade and refuge from the scorching sun and high temperatures to traders, pilgrims, royal hunting parties and troops on the march.

Perhaps the most important motivation for commissioning the building of a stepwell was the desire to gain merit. The gift of water was the most noble act of all and this is repeatedly reflected in the writings of the ancient sages, one of which states '...of all the charitable acts, the giving of water is the most superior because water gives satisfaction to all living beings. It is for this reason that men build water buildings, so they may gain happiness in this world and the next' (Oza, 2005, p. 43). According to Agni Purana, 'one who consecrates a reservoir of water (acquires) in a single day a merit ten crore (or, hundred million) times more than one who performs thousands of Ashvamedha Yagna (the horse sacrifice). Such a person ascends on to heaven in the (celestial) vehicle and rejoices (there). He never goes to hell' (Agni Purana, 1967, Vol. 27, Part 1, p. 178).

With the establishment of British administration in the nineteenth century and the introduction of modern technologies of managing water resources such as taps, pumps and tube wells, the stepwells lost their usefulness and became obsolete, a reminder of the times gone by.

Until recently the stepwells were among the least visited monuments in India. Because they were generally located in remote areas and in small villages and isolated towns, few people were aware of their existence. These structures were seen as utilitarian buildings, in contrast to temples and pilgrimage sites, which were imbued with religious meaning and were frequented by pious Hindus.

WATER STRUCTURES

From ancient times, there existed numerous water structures like lakes, *kund*s (ponds), wells and stepwells. *Sarovar*s were ponds generally constructed of stone or with mud walls on all sides, while a *kund* is a pond found in the vicinity of a temple. Stepwells are different from stepped ponds. The latter was built in the vicinity or adjacent to a temple and was used for ritual bathing prior to the performance of ceremonies. Ordinary wells found all over the land are simple structures and were generally circular in shape; water from these was drawn by lowering a pot using a rope. The building of ordinary wells was less expensive than the stepwells as is evident from the popular saying '*panch kuva barabar ek vav*' meaning one stepwell is equivalent to five wells.

The stepwell is referred to in Sanskrit as *vapi* or *vapika* and in Gujarati as vav or *bauli*.[1] It is a rectangular or octagonal structure containing a flight of steps leading down to the water (Howard, 1967, pp. 227–30). In contrast to ordinary wells, the stepwells did not require a rope or any other device to draw water. One could simply go down the steps and obtain water. In order to reach the water level in the well, several storeys were constructed. Some had three, five, seven or nine storeys referred to as *kutas*. At frequent intervals, there were landing platforms and galleries that served as resting areas.[2] Some stepwells have a *mandapa* or pavilion with an entrance hall called *mandapika*. Thus, vavs, in contrast to ordinary wells, were more elaborate structures, often multi-storeyed. They also differed from wells in that they often contain elaborate decorations and embellishments on the walls, which were profusely decorated with designs of flowers, vines, leaves and animals. The niches and platform pillars contain sculptural depictions of gods and goddesses.

Recent research indicates that the building of stepwells was not limited to Gujarat. In Rajasthan, a large number of stepwells were built between the eighth and the eleventh centuries. Notable among them are the stepwells of Ossian, Abhineri, Bhinmal, Vasantgadh, Nadol, Sevasi, Udaipur and Bundi. In Delhi, Ugrasena ki Baoli, Gandhak ki Baoli and Raja ki Baoli are worth mentioning. Stepwells were also built in Punjab and Haryana. Some of these stepwells were commissioned by women.

---

[1] In Marathi and Hindi, it is known as *vavdi* and *bavdi*, or *baori*. There is an ancient text dealing with the construction of stepwells known as *Vapi Shilpa Shastra*.

[2] In Saurashtra, stepwells which had platforms and landing areas at intervals were known as *nalvali vav* or *naladi*.

Different Types of Stepwells

One can find a classification and description of different kinds of stepwells in ancient texts such as Rajvallabha, which differentiates between the four main types of stepwells:

Nanda: a stepwell with one entrance
Bhadra: a stepwell with two entrances
Jaya: a stepwell with three entrances
Vijaya: a stepwell with four entrances

Of these, Vijaya is the most elaborate and is called 'Dirdhika', meaning the length of 300 bows. A living stepwell is so named because it is never devoid of water and provides a perennial source of water. The stepwells were generally built using mortar, stone, brick, rubble, stucco and occasionally even marble.

ANCIENT WELLS IN HISTORY AND MYTHOLOGY

While Lothal and Dholavira in Gujarat attest to thousands of years of water engineering skills, examples of the earliest vavs date back to at least the sixth century C.E.

In Kulu valley in Himachal Pradesh, in the village of Nirmad there are said to have been seven large and seven small stepwells providing water to seven *jati*s or sub-castes. Now only the four large ones remain. Of these, one is in Lalteba. According to folk traditions, this was built by the Pandavas. There are other numerous water buildings associated with the Pandavas both in Gujarat and Maharashtra. There are also a number of water buildings in Mandi. The Rani of Sundarnagar is said to have built Shivabavadi near the Maha Mrityunjaya temple.

Ordinary citizens also built various types of water buildings to meet their daily needs for water. It is said that Motisar pond in Surendranagar *jilla* (district) was built by a Vanjara in remembrance of a dog named Moti who had shown great loyalty towards and had sacrificed his life for his master.

Stepwells were also built to provide water to irrigate the fields. Thus, the historic inscriptions and edicts dealing with land grants make several references to stepwells, many of which were named after architectural features or important landmarks or their patrons.

ORIGIN AND EARLY HISTORY OF STEPWELLS

In 1922, excavations carried out on the banks of the river Indus unearthed the remains of the Indus Valley Civilisation dating back to circa 2500 B.C.E. These excavations revealed the existence of large public baths and reservoirs which, while not stepwells, resembled the later stepped ponds used for ritual bathing. Excavations carried out at the site of ancient Harappan towns reveal the presence of sophisticated systems of drainage, wells and tanks. The evidence derived from the excavations at the Harappan site of Dholavira in Gujarat show that the inhabitants had devised a complex system for collecting and storing rainwater in reservoirs. This provides evidence that from the earliest times, Indians had developed systems for water conservation and management (Hooja n.d., p. 1). At Mohenjodaro and other Indus Valley Civilisation sites, excavations have yielded evidence of individual wells which provided water to the residents (ibid., p. 2). These represent the precursor or prototype of later water architecture.

According to archaeologists, there once may have been as many as 700 wells in the city of Mohenjodaro alone. Dholavira, in Kutch where excavations have been carried out since 1990 is the most recent of the sites from the Indus Civilisation and is said to have flourished over 4,500 years ago. Findings reveal the existence of a well planned water system and a water tank built of stone. According to Bisht who carried out these excavations, there once existed more than 16 reservoirs in Dholavira, which were sophisticated devices to collect and store rainwater (Possehl, 2004, p. 70). Excavations carried out at Lothal in Gujarat have unearthed a well constructed from burnt bricks.

While archeological excavations of pre-historic sites are providing evidence of wells and reservoirs, we also have written documentary evidence of their existence from over 2,000 years ago. A type of stepwell is said to have been constructed as early as the reign of Ashoka in the third century B.C.E. The seventh edict on the Delhi–Topra Pillar refers to a 'flight of steps' (nimsidha; Hultzsch, 1969, p. 130).

In Gujarat, the reign of the Solanki rulers (circa 942–1244 C.E.) was regarded as a golden age during which they patronised the construction of numerous temples and stepwells. The existence of a stone quarry at Motipura, near Dabhoi supports the view that the stone for the construction of the wells was obtained from here. While the Solanki kings were responsible for the construction of a large number of temples, it is their wives who were primarily the patrons of stepwells, thereby alleviating the water problems for their subjects. From the many inscriptions it is evident that many of Gujarat's stepwells are named after female goddesses such as Mata Bhavani, Amba Mata and Ma Ankol.

There are also some references to stepwells in *Baburnama*, the autobiography of Babur, the founder of the Mughal dynasty, which was established in 1526 C.E. It is stated that Babur who was deeply interested in stepwells requested Gujarati builders to construct two stepwells which he commissioned. In referring to these, he used the word '*vahin*' which means vav.

References to stepwells are found in ancient Sanskrit texts and also the writings of English and European travellers and administrators. These stepwells constructed in Gujarat and the neighbouring region of Rajasthan, are unique structures not found anywhere else in the world. According to John Marshall, 'there are no other wells in the world, that structurally, and decoratively, can compare with these stepwells of Western India, and it was because their builders were content to keep the established traditions of the country that they were able to attain such perfection' (1928, p. 614). This was possible because both under the Hindu dynasties, as well as during the Islamic period, the construction of these wells was in the hands of the Somparas or hereditary caste of masons who carried on this tradition from generation to generation. These craftsmen faithfully conformed to the traditions and strict guidelines provided in the canonical texts on architecture and sculpture such as Shilpa Shastras and the Vastu Shastras. Writing on the marvels of these water structures, James Burgess states, 'so long as the water in the well was kept fresh, nothing could be cooler during the heat of the day in early summer than these rock-hewn chambers, and doubtless they were often occupied for an hour or two during seasons of recreation' (1896, p. 47).

James Tod, during the course of his travels through western India, encountered stepwells which he refers to as 'baoris'. Describing them he writes,

> We may include in the domestic structures, those useful and ornamental excavations called baoris, which serve both as reservoirs and abodes in the hot season. Some of these are on a gigantic scale, and may be described generally as circular pits, from twenty to fifty feet in diameter, and of depth proportionate to the springs. Suites of chambers, storey below storey, approached by a staircase, surround them from the surface to the waters's edge, which in hot weather, form delightful retreats for the chiefs and their families (Tod, 1839, p. 133).

The stepwells, as described by Tod, were used by royal hunting parties and troops on the move who sought refuge and rest in these cool chambers to escape the intense heat of the day and drink the cool water. Tod in his annals also comments on the fact that the *baori*s or reservoirs of water withstood invasions and upheavals. They survived even in times when there was wanton destruction or neglect of other structures. While Hindu temples may have suffered destruction and desecration at the hands of fanatical Muslim invaders, most stepwells were apparently left untouched. This may be attributed to the utilitarian function these stepwells served and that it was in the interest of the invaders to leave them alone to gain support from the local people.

In addition to the 'ruins of a bowree' in the old fort at Puttun, Tod also mentions a reservoir in Girnar and the stepwell in Ghumli which he wrote, '…affords some notion of the munificence of purse and spirit of the ancient Jaitwas' (ibid.).

Mention is made of stepwells by a number of other Europeans who travelled through western India from the seventeenth to the nineteenth century such as Thévenot, Captain Le Grand Jacob, Rousselet and Briggs. In their writings they provide interesting information about these stepwells, which aroused their curiosity and impressed them with their ingenious architectural features and beauty.

Thevenot, who was born in Paris in 1633, was an ardent student of geography and natural resources. He travelled through Gujarat and has left behind a detailed description of the Dada Harir stepwell in Ahmedabad. He writes, 'Within the city of Ahmedabad, there is a lovely well, the figure of it is an oblong square; it is covered with seven arches of freestone, that much adorn it.' He goes on to state that, '… the water of it rises from a spring, and it was up to the middle of the fourth level when I went down. Several little boys at that time [were] swimming in it from one end to the other amongst the pillars' (Thevenot, 1665, p. 16).

Le Grand Jacob in 1837 encountered the stepwell in Ghumli and states, '… nothing remains as witness of its former state save an insignificant temple near the eastern wall … a splendid well, itself worthy of description' (cited by Rousselet, 1876, p. 60).

Rousselet in his account makes a special mention of a 'baoli' at Tintoui and states that this 'antique cistern known by the name of baolis which one may class among the most interesting monuments of the country.' He goes on to say, 'when they are found, as at Tintoui in a desert place, I know few monuments that strike the traveler more, when entering for the first time, he penetrates gradually into the mysterious galleries' (Rousselet, 1876, pp. 134–35).

James MacMurdo, in his travel through Saurashtra in the nineteenth century, wrote, 'We passed two bowries of very ancient structure, but originally intended for the accommodation of travelers' (1977).

Henry Briggs gives us a fascinating account of his travels across

Gujarat and Saurashtra. He writes 'At an early hour, accompanied by a newly-formed acquaintance, set out for the Kolapur gate; and after a ride of half a mile over heavy ground heading due north-east, we arrived at the handsome and famed well, known to the natives as Dhyi Hari Ki Bauri or Nurse Hari's well, said to be miniature counterpart of the one at Adalaj' (Briggs, 1849, p. 217). In his travelogue he narrates a legend commonly prevalent during this time. The legend states that Resham, who belonged to the Garasiya tribe and upon her conversion to Islam came to be known by the name of Dhyi Hari, was determined to attract the attention of the Sultan. She employed amorous intrigue and obtained entry into the harem of Sultan Begada as a nurse of one of the royal children. Successful in her objective she amassed enormous wealth and possessed two priceless diamond anklets, one of which she sold to pay for this stepwell. The legend goes on to state that the other she threw away into the well (ibid.).

The stepwells of Gujarat thus represent a unique form of water architecture, which is both functional in nature as well as aesthetically beautiful. An examination of these stepwells constructed under the patronage of Hindu and Muslim dynasties reveals the unique attitude of religious tolerance and a spirit of assimilation rarely witnessed elsewhere. These stepwells successfully transcend religious differences and sectarian conflicts.

4

The Woman Factor

From about the seventh to the nineteenth centuries, stepwells were constructed to provide a year round source of water for people and animals. Some were elaborate and imposing multi- storeyed structures while others were purely functional and utilitarian, modest in size and lacking much ornamentation and decoration. It is estimated that of the several hundred stepwells in Gujarat, perhaps one-fifth or more were built or commissioned by women—queens, women of the royal families, wives of prosperous merchants, mothers and daughters and even servant girls and prostitutes.[1] Many of these stepwells contain inscriptions which provide valuable information regarding the name of the donor, date or year of construction, the motivation and purpose behind its construction and detailed genealogies of the royal families to which some of these women belonged. These inscriptions thus give the historical information in the absence of which the women of the past would remain forgotten and invisible.

A large number of these stepwells were also built to honour a local or family goddess or female deity such as Bhavani, Ashapuri, Sindhwai, Ankolmata, Shikottari, Kankavati, Matri, Bhadrakali, Sitala and many others.

---

[1] See description of Adi-Kadi ni vav, Singer Stepwell and Vaishya ni vav in Chapter 5 for stepwells built by women of the lower classes.

Of the hundreds of stepwells in Gujarat studied by archeologists, at least 17 were commissioned by women patrons or built to honour them. From the perspective of architectural style and form, ornamentation and inscriptions these stepwells reflect women's agency and participation in art and architecture. They are expressions of women's unique sensibilities, their pre-eminent concerns and their striving to challenge the notion that women's lives are insignificant, irrelevant and doomed to oblivion. Through the patronage of stepwells, these women were demanding a place in the pages of history and vying for immortality.

ASSOCIATION OF WATER WITH GODDESS AND MOTHER

From the dawn of human history, an association was made between woman and water. According to Hindu conception, the 'waters are female; they are the maternal, procreative aspect of the absolute' (Zimmer, 1946, p. 90). Water became identified with woman, the mother and the forces of creation.

Thus, from the beginning of time, women have been associated with water and rivers were perceived as female because they provided life-giving water. The earliest civilisations in the world originated on the banks of rivers such as the Euphrates and the Tigris, the Nile, the Yangtze and the Indus. Over time, rivers came to be regarded as sacred. In Gujarat and Saurashtra also, the major rivers like Narmada, Tapi and Mahi were revered and worshipped as mothers, and temples and shrines were constructed on their banks to honour them. In the villages of Bharuch, Shihor, Tilakvada and Vyas, Narmada *mata* or goddess Narmada is depicted in the temples as riding a crocodile. In the Kutch region of Gujarat, there is a temple dedicated to Ashapuri (Asara) on the oceanfront.

On the banks of the Bhadar river near Junagadh is a temple dedicated to the goddess Bhadrai, while the Gomtiji temple on the banks of river Gomti and Chandrabhagaji temple on the river Chandrabhaga are dedicated to the two goddesses. The term 'Sindhvai' means born of 'Sindhu' and she is the deity associated with the Sindhu sea. According to Pathak, a niche in a well on the outskirts of Patan is her abode (1997, p. 212). Then there is the *devi* 'Varudi' or 'Vaduchi' who too is associated with water. It is probable that this water goddess was believed to protect boatmen of the Kharvas and Koli communities from drowning. Unjha, Rupal, Radhampur, Bharuch, Kutch and Amreli are the centres of worship of this goddess. Other local goddesses associated with water include Shikottari and Vahanamati Mata.

Some scholars opine that the temple/shrine on Samudra Tapi Sangam is dedicated to Sangamatridevi. According to popular lore, a wealthy merchant of Vallabhipur, Sheth Akhéchand Vanik's ships were being lost at sea. His wife Leelavati, a pious lady, appealed to the goddess Amba who salvaged the shipwrecks with her trident. Boatsmen refer to her as Vahanavatidevi (goddess of seafaring vessels). She is depicted as an infant with 20 arms sitting in the lap of Mahamaya in the form of a square red stone in the courtyard of the temple of the *devi* (ibid., p. 213).

Shikottari Mata's shrines are found in many village stepwells in Gujarat and she is given offerings of white rice and sweets. One such shrine is found at the entrance of the stepwell in the village of Chatral. The shrine contains two images of the goddess Shikottari (ibid., p. 264). Another sculptural image of this local goddess is in the entrance of the stepwell in Mandala village, which contains nine sculptures revered as Jaladevi, the goddess associated with waters. According to Pathak, each image of the goddess has her right arm raised up to the breast as though holding oars while her waist is bent. Other shrines of the goddess are found in Chanasma district in Kamboi, Kadi, Chotila and Dabka village.

Near Halvad in Surendranagar district, there is a village named Sundarei where the goddess Sundari is the patron deity of several communities, namely the Koli boatmen, Kapol Vaniya, Sorathia Vaniya, and Kanodia Brahmins. In ancient times, Sundari was a well known port and sailors travelled from here to distant places. There are temples dedicated to this deity in Prabhas Patan and Vallabhipura (Pathak, 1997, p. 214).

There is a stepwell in Karkhadi village of Padra district which has a sculpture of Mahishasura Mardini. She is depicted as riding a lion and near the mouth of the lion there is a demon. Near the goddess is an image of a long *naga* or serpent. According to Pathak, it is probable that at some time a serpent lived in the waters of the well and was worshipped as a deity (ibid., p. 215).

In Dakor, in the ancient and well known stepwell of Umreth is a shrine of Bhadrakali, a popular form of *devi*. She is worshipped by her devotees to acquire wealth and prosperity.

WOMEN AS PATRONS OF WATER ARCHITECTURE

There are thousands of stepwells in Gujarat and Rajasthan, some elegant and monumental while others are austere structures without embellishment and decoration. History and legend link many of these stepwells to women. The primary focus of my research has been to explore those stepwells which were commissioned by women, or constructed to honour and commemorate some female—mother, wife, daughter, courtesan, pious women, servant girls or goddesses.

One may ask the intriguing question: why did women commission these different types of water buildings—wells, stepwells, ponds and reservoirs? What motivated them to become patrons of art and architecture?

From time immemorial, the gift of water was regarded as a deeply pious act. According to the ancient texts, those who built wells and stepwells to quench the thirst of humans and animals acquired great religious merit and gained fame and immortality. It is for this reason that women, and men paid for the construction of stepwells. Furthermore, the practice of digging wells in remembrance of the dead was widely prevalent and this is corroborated by both epigraphic and oral tradition. Wells were built to honour a deceased relative.

Some of the best known wells in Gujarat, namely the Rani ni vav built by Queen Udayamati and the stepwell in Adalaj attributed to Queen Rudabai, were built under the patronage of widowed queens to honour their deceased husbands. This religious act is referred to in Sanskrit texts as 'istapurta' (a pious work or sacrifice which confers merit).

Women's patronage of water buildings can also be understood in view of the fact that the responsibility of fetching water fell on womenfolk. Thus, the building of wells represented a noble activity which benefited a large number of women, while conferring great merit on the donor.

The inscriptions found on the wells provide detailed information about the date of construction, name of the donor, the genealogy of their families, the purpose of building the well, the cost of construction and, sometimes, the name of the chief craftsman. It is from these inscriptions that historians are able to piece together facts about these women donors who otherwise would remain obscure and overlooked in the historical records of that time.

Women's patronage of these wells also challenges and questions the existing and long-lasting stereotypes of their passivity, the myth that women were silent spectators on the stage of history, not active participants. It is tempting to suggest that one of the chief motivations for commissioning wells was precisely to insert themselves into history to prevent being forgotten. They wanted to bestow their name to posterity. Various inscriptions and written records challenge the previously held assumptions about women's passivity and testify to women's patronage of art in India. Dehejia's research on women as artists, patrons and painters reveals the startling and, until recently, little known fact that at Bharhut, nearly two-thirds of the donors were women. This is quite significant because it indicates that women were independently wealthy and owned property and were, therefore, free to commission works of art and architecture[2] (Dehejia, 1997, p. 9).

When women become patrons of art and architecture, they call into question and challenge the prevailing notions of their passivity. It also enables them to exert some power and establish their separate

[2] Inscriptions from a number of stepwells commissioned by women make a specific mention of the amount of money expended by the women for the construction. These include the Bai Harir, Badula and Roho stepwells.

identity in a patriarchal society. Women's agency in art also had other important implications: they had greater control over the subject matter of the art. As donors or patrons, they were able to exercise some measure of discretion in the selection of the images as well as make architectural choices. While the art in the stepwells followed and conformed to the guidelines provided by the texts like the *Shilpa Shastras* (the treatises on architecture and sculpture), the stepwell art nevertheless reveals the unique individuality of the women and shows that they succeeded in taking some liberties with the themes depicted. Within the established guidelines the patrons could, and did, exercise some measure of freedom and autonomy regarding the subject matter and the iconography. They succeeded in representing women's perspectives and special concerns. The stepwell art also depicts the local goddesses, *apsaras*, the waters, aquatic animals and birds, the identification with the world of nature, the Saptamatrikas or seven mothers, *Navagraha* or the nine planets, scenes of domestic life, maternal love and the preoccupation with women's beauty and loveliness.

It is tempting to put forward the hypothesis that the art produced under women's patronage has a more sensuous and delicate quality to it. It is highly refined and exudes tenderness and a marked elegance, most noticeable in the Queen's stepwell at Patan, Rudabai's stepwell at Adalaj and Dada Harir's stepwell at Ahmedabad. While the pre-eminent gods of Hinduism—Shiva, Vishnu and Brahma are featured in some of the stepwells, it is mainly the veneration of the local goddesses that is the focal point of the art. It is also worth mentioning that many of the female deities who were worshipped in the stepwells were non-Aryan or pre-Aryan and as such represent aboriginal and non-Brahmanical origins. These include goddesses like Kali, Durga, Sitala and Ambika. This may suggest a covert challenge to the Hindu patriarchal traditions. Thus, one could suggest that the art of the stepwells is more 'feminine' and represents a departure and contrast from the art found in Hindu temples.

With further excavations of stepwells and the deciphering of the inscriptions contained in them, we are discovering that many stepwells were commissioned by women in Rajasthan and other parts of India too. Examples include, the *baoli* built by women in Punjab and Haryana. A notable example is the stepwell from the mid-nineteenth century at Khanna (Ludhiana district in Punjab) attributed to a woman named Dhyan Kaur. Another stepwell in Sirsa is said to have been commissioned in the seventeenth century by Ratno, the childless wife of Gurdial Khatri (Parihar, 1999, p. 63).

Stepwells were also a focal point of women's rites and rituals which shed light on women's religious lives—the everyday rituals centred around fertility, desire for many sons, the health and well being of their husbands and family, freedom from illness and disease, desire for long life and the propitiation of local goddesses. Over time, many of the stepwells were seen as the abode of certain female deities and contained shrines (*thanak*) built to honour female deities such as Shikottari Mata, Amba Mata, Bhavani Mata, Ankol Mata, and Utvali Mata.

WOMEN AND SPACE

From the very earliest of times, in virtually all societies, women have been relegated and confined to the 'domestic' sphere while men's activities link them to the 'public' realm. The underlying assumption here is that it is their biological role, the fact that they give birth to children, which would explain their being identified with the private realm.

According to more recent feminist theory and critique, however, this association of women with the 'private' and domestic realm was not biologically determined, but more likely a result of the culturally constructed role of women as the primary nurturers and caregivers in the family. Women are responsible for the care of children and the elderly, for the upkeep of home and the preparation of food—all time consuming and demanding activities. In stark contrast, men are freer to move out of the domestic and engage in the public realm. Until recently it was the men who participated in politics, warfare, art, architecture, literature and government. Being confined and restricted to the home implied that women had fewer or no opportunities to move into the public realm, to establish cross-cutting networks of support and to seek and exercise power.

The stepwells are in a sense unique because they provided women a socially legitimated opportunity to move out of the domestic (albeit just for a few hours daily) and step out into the public domain. This enabled them to escape the oppression of their daily lives, the exploitation and restrictions they experienced in a deeply patriarchal society where they were forever subject to the authority of the husbands, the in-laws and the social constraints placed on them by a conservative and rigid society. Thus, the stepwells where women went to fetch water daily afforded them a brief measure of freedom and autonomy. It allowed them to express their sorrows and frustrations and perhaps seek solace and support from other women (see Chapter 8 on folklore for a more detailed discussion of this). The wells and stepwells provided women with a measure of social freedom and served as what Rapoport aptly calls a 'safety valve' (1969, p. 25).

In a traditional Indian marriage where a young girl is dramatically uprooted from her childhood home and the protection of her parents and friends, the stepwell could be seen as a place for her to forge new friendships. This possibility offered a temporary but, nevertheless, liberating moment for her. The few minutes or hours of leisure at the stepwell offered her the opportunity to express her fantasies, to imagine the unimaginable, and to momentarily enjoy the freedom of her childhood. She could escape her confining environment and the restrictions placed on her movements and enjoy a few hours with other women. The stepwell served as a substitute for her *piyara* or childhood.

The rules of social segregation in traditional societies clearly stipulated separate areas of play and work for men and women. Women were relegated generally to the inner and darker areas of the home, away from the gaze of the opposite sex while men occupied the sun-lit courtyard, open verandahs and open spaces. The women often lacked spatial and psychological space of their own. The stepwells and wells offered them that space where they came to laugh and cry, to share their joys and sorrows, and to while away an hour or two and enjoy leisure, something they rarely possessed. The songs and folklore emanating from these encounters provide a glimpse into the inner lives of women in a gendered society about which we know so little and which give us invaluable insight into the lived experience of these women (see Chapter 8 on women and folklore.)

An intriguing question comes to mind with respect to the spoken and unspoken rules and restrictions relating to the use of the stepwells—'Who had access to them?' If royal hunting parties, itinerant traders and travellers and troops on the march utilised these stepwells as a resting place to escape the heat of the day, did they encroach on the territory we call 'women's space'? While there are no clear and definitive answers to this question, one can surmise that in the early hours of the morning and at dusk, the stepwells were mainly the territorial domain of the women who went to fetch water there. Thus, society over centuries had effectively generated its own rules regarding the use of stepwells.[3] During the few hours that women came to fetch water, these wells served spatially, physically, spiritually and psychologically as the exclusive domain of women and, by and large, males and strangers stayed away during that time. The encounters with strangers on the way to the well were not unknown. Though infrequent, they often form the subject matter of folk songs which deal with romantic liaisons resulting from such chance encounters. Literature also hints at the consequences of illicit love affairs carried out on the banks of rivers, wells and stepwells and the tragedies which ensued when boundaries were breached.

In the nineteenth century when stepwells became obsolete and no longer served their original purpose, women once again repossessed them, establishing a claim on these structures and transformed them into shrines for the worship of local mother goddesses. In so doing,

---

[3] Under these rigid rules, untouchables and members of the lowest caste were prohibited from drawing water from the wells and stepwells and compelled to go elsewhere for water.

they asserted their right to carve out some space for themselves and create their own identities.

WOMEN'S RITES AND RITUALS

Women in the Hindu Brahmanical tradition were prohibited by the Shastras or sacred texts from worshipping certain deities or performing certain ceremonial rituals. The worship of the main gods of Hinduism—Vishnu, Shiva and Brahma—was enjoined in the canonical texts and specific ceremonials were prescribed for this purpose. Women, however, were debarred from the ceremonial worship of these deities, from learning the Vedas or performing the hymn to the sun (Gayatri Mantra). This clearly reflected their inferior position in society and the perception of their ritual impurity. Consequently, they evolved their own rites and rituals.

These rituals developed and practised by the womenfolk primarily centred on the worship and veneration of goddesses or *devis*, manifestations of 'Shakti', the feminine principle in the cosmos. The worship of these local goddesses varied from village to village, and from one region to another and took myriad forms. However, they represent a powerful tradition of female power, going back to the beginnings of Indian civilisation. The excavations at the sites of the Indus Valley Civilisation dating back to over 4,000 years have unearthed many terracotta figurines of the mother goddess and this tradition continues to survive to the present day.

Since time immemorial, women have performed rites and ceremonies near temples, rivers, stepwells and ponds to propitiate the deities to obtain fertility and to secure the health, prosperity and long life of their husbands. These religious observances were performed by women only. They made offerings of food, milk, flowers, coconuts, turmeric, and red lac to propitiate the goddess and to ask for her blessings. It was a common practice in the past for newly wed couples to visit the local stepwell to receive blessings before setting up their household. This practice has survived into the present day. Another of these rituals takes place on the fifth day of the bright half of Bhadrapad (August–September) to atone for sins committed unknowingly. On this day, women go to a river, well or some other sacred spot to cleanse their teeth with the leaves of the Aghada plant and bathe. They then collect some stones and worship them as rishis or sages. Women, who have no male children, take a vow to worship the goddess Pithori on the last day of Shravan (July–August) to secure the blessings of a son. Young unmarried girls desiring suitable husbands carry clay pots containing freshly sprouted grain. They make offerings of these to the goddess. The grain is symbolic of fertility and new life.

The goddess Sitala is depicted in many of the stepwells. Women seek the protection of this goddess of smallpox on the seventh day of the dark half of Shravan (July–August) and observe the vow of 'Sitala-satem' to secure their protection for their children (Enthoven and Jackson, 1989, p. 283).

About a month after her delivery, a ceremony called 'Zarmazaryan' is performed when the woman is taken to a neighbouring well or stream to fetch water. In the vicinity of the well, five small mounds of sand are made which are daubed with red lac. After this, a *ghee* lamp is lit and seven small betel nuts are given as offerings to the water. This is followed by the breaking of a coconut, which is thrown into the water, and the woman returns to her home with a jar filled with the waters which have just been consecrated. On the return journey, she distributes the betel nuts to women who suffer from barrenness for it is commonly believed that this will cure them of their condition and result in conception (ibid., p. 289).

Thus, the stepwells served as a site for the performance of rituals and ceremonies directed at the local goddesses to ensure the fertility and well being of the women. They fulfilled an immediate and compelling need for the women, not just for water essential for survival and domestic use, but more importantly to alleviate their day-to-day concerns centred around fertility, children, husbands and happiness. They came here to restore the order in 'their' universe and to renew themselves.

5

Description of Individual Stepwells

The history of Gujarat can be classified into the following periods:

1. The Kshatrapa Period (c. 23–400 C.E.)
2. Maitraka Period (c. 470–788 C.E.)
3. Chaulukya Period (c. 942–1304 C.E.)
   a. Solanki Rule (c. 942–1244 C.E.)
   b. Vaghela Rule (c. 1244–1304 C.E.)
4. Sultanate Period (c. 1305–1500 C.E.)
5. Mughal Period, British Rule and Post-Independence Period (c. 1500 C.E. to the present)

KSHATRAPA PERIOD

There are no known surviving vavs from this period. However, a stone inscription of the Kshatrapa Rudrasimha dated 181 C.E. records that the military chief Rudrabhuti dug and constructed a stepwell in the village of Rasopadra (Shelat, 2011, p. 50).

MAITRAKA PERIOD

The earliest stepwell in Gujarat is said to have been constructed in the Maitraka age in Saurashtra at Jhilani (550 C.E.). However, there are very few extant remains of stepwells from this very early period. Some years ago, Gaudani identified an 'L' shaped stepwell at Dhank which has decorated carved niches on one wall and may belong to this period. Not much information is available regarding this structure, or its builder (Shastri, 2000, p. 339).

There are two stepwells from the Maitraka period associated with women patrons. The Jhala ni vav in Saurashtra is said to have been built in the sixth century by the wife of one Chandrashaila Damor. Unfortunately, very little information is available on the woman who commissioned this well. Chandrashaila Damor's wife is also credited with being the patron of the Manjusar ni vav, also in Saurashtra. It was probably built in the early seventh century.

CHAULUKYA PERIOD

This period covers the Solanki and Vaghela rule in Gujarat, which was followed by Islamic rule or the Sultanate period. A large number of stepwells were built during the rule of these dynasties between 942 and 1304 C.E. This was the golden age of art and architecture. Anhilwara Patan was the capital of the Solankis whose important rulers include Moolraj, Bhimdev, Jaisinh, Kumarapala, Visdev, Karnadev, and Siddharaja.

The distinctive feature of the stepwells built during the Solanki age was that they were mainly built of stone. The existence of a stone quarry at Motipura, near Dabhoi supports the view that it supplied the stone for the construction of the stepwells. These stepwells were elaborate structures with ornamentation and embellishment. Male and female deities occupied a prominent place in their art. The stepwells of this period are also unique in that the nine planets (Navagraha) and the Saptamatrikas (seven mother goddesses) were depicted only during the Solanki period.

Another unique characteristic of the Solanki rule is their attitude of tolerance and their religious eclecticism. The Solanki rulers were Shaivites, followers of Shiva, but their buildings honour the many gods of Hinduism and pay special homage to Vishnu and Devi.

Some of the best known and preserved stepwells of this period include the following.

Patan ni vav (Rani ni vav)

The most majestic and elegant of all the stepwells in Gujarat is the Rani ni vav or Queen's Stepwell in Patan. It was commissioned by Queen Udayamati, wife of Bhimdev I in 1063 C.E. It is a seven storeyed structure which was restored in 1986. Chapter 7 of this book is devoted to a detailed description of this stepwell in Patan.

Adi Kadi ni vav

This stepwell in Junagadh district is said to have been built in the eleventh century C.E. by the Chudasama Rajputs for Adi and Kadi. According to popular legend, Adi and Kadi, two young servant girls were sacrificed so there would be water in the well. A more plausible explanation is that the stepwell was named after Adi and Kadi who fetched water from it. To commemorate them, people still hang cloth and bangles on a nearby tree. There is a popular saying 'Adi Kadi ni vav ane navghan kuvo, je na juwe te jivto muvo' (Anyone who has not seen the vav and the well is like a living corpse). This stepwell, carved entirely from hard rock, is 123 feet deep and there are 166 steps leading down to the water. Parimal Rupani, a Junagadh historian, believes that in fact Adi and Kadi were two separate stepwells and that the latter is still buried under the ground. According to him the structure that is visible today is really the Adi stepwell.

Ma Ankol ni vav (also known as Davad ni vav)

This stepwell is located in the village of Davad in the Sabarkantha district. While no inscription has been found on it, a text written in the past century titled Davad Purana says the stepwell was built in the eleventh century C.E. by a merchant named Anko after whom it was named. However, there seems no clear consensus on who built this stepwell. Some scholars hold the view that it was commissioned by Queen Hansoldevi, the wife of Siddharaja Solanki. The stepwell contains a shrine honouring the local goddess Vihat Mata, depicted as slaying the buffalo demon. This may represent Mahishasura Mardini. This image was given the name of Ankol Mata. There is an inscription in the shrine with a date of 1249 and a mention of 'Davad'. There are sculptural decorations in the stepwell of erotic scenes (*maithuna*), Kirtimukhas (or victory faces) and floral designs. There are several representations of the goddess most notably of her dancing, standing, and holding a drum. Scenes of daily life include depiction of sexual intercourse and that of a woman serving water from a pitcher to a seated couple. The amorous and explicitly sexual scenes also depict women engaged in sexual intercourse with animals and convey a sense of humour and playfulness.

Dumral Bhagol ni vav

Built under the patronage of Queen Minaldevi, mother of King Siddharaja during the Solanki and Vaghela age in the eleventh century C.E., this well is situated in the town of Nadiad in Kheda district and contains an inscription in Sanskrit. This is a four-storeyed structure.

Vaikya vav

Located in Ghumli in the Jamnagar district of Gujarat, this twelfth century stepwell is said to have been built by Queen Rudadevi, though other scholars believe it was commissioned by Raja Khetaji of the Jethwa dynasty.[1] It contains an inscription in Sanskrit.

Ganga vav

Built in 1169 C.E. and located in Wadhwan, this is now a protected monument. The Archeological Department of India has conferred

---

[1] Jethwa is the name of a Kshatriya Rajput clan which once ruled over Porbandar, Morvi and Ghumli.

this status on this stepwell because of its unique architectural features which include an unusual pyramidal roof on top, instead of the usual dome and the beautiful ornamental gate which still stands today.

Madhav vav or Madhavav

In the present day town of Wadhwan, known in ancient times as Vardhamanpur, in Surendranagar district, there are three well known stepwells, celebrated in folksongs and popular lore. These include Madha vav, Ganga vav and the third is known as Lakha vav. Madha vav is the only one of these three associated with women. It is a seven-storeyed structure containing sculptures of gods and goddesses, Saptamatrikas, nine planets, reincarnations of Lord Vishnu and erotic sculptures. There are two inscriptions in the Madhavav. One contains a narrative of Tashamadevi, the daughter of the Nagar minister Sodhal; it states that Sidhu and Tashamadevi were probably the parents of Madhav (Barot, 2006, p. 100).

A Sanskrit inscription found in Madhavav states that it was built in 1294 C.E. at the end of the Vaghela rule. It is a two-storeyed structure built in stone and is said to have been commissioned by Madhav, a Brahmin minister of Karnadeva II Vaghela, in honour of his father and mother (Oza, 2005, p. 36). Madhavav is renowned for the tale of love and sacrifice associated with it.

According to a popular legend, when there was no water in the stepwell for many years, the astrologer was summoned who predicted that the vav would have water only if a son and his wife would sacrifice their life. The people of the village were stunned by this prophecy but when the young prince heard of this, he and his wife showed their willingness to offer their lives. They were a young couple with an infant child. The wife sent a message to her parents: 'Tell my father and mother to come here in haste with my bridal clothes.' The parents complied and the young couple dressed in their wedding finery started to descend the steps of the well. When they reached the seventh step, the stepwell filled with water (ibid., p. 37). Thus, the selfless couple drowned and gave their lives to ensure that the stepwell would once again have sufficient water (for the translation of this legend, see Chapter 8 on folklore).

Mata Bhavani ni vav

This 'Nanda' stepwell is located in Asarva village of Ahmedabad. There is a description of it in the text *Mirat-i-Ahmadi*. On the basis of its architectural features, Dr Burgess is of the opinion that it was constructed prior to the founding of the city of Ahmedabad and represents the earliest extant example of Hindu architecture (Burgess, 1902) prior to the settlement of Ahmedabad. The pillars and steps of the *vav* are Hindu in style. However, near the first landing of this stepwell is an exquisite screen on the wall. Sankalia has suggested that this cannot belong to the pre-Muslim period as these types of perforated screen walls were introduced only during the Muslim period (Ibid., 1941, p. 72). According to scholars, the stepwell was probably constructed during the reign of Karnadev, (1083–1093 C.E.), the Chaulukya king who is also credited with founding the ancient city of Karnavati. Other scholars believe that the stepwell was commissioned by Queen Minaldevi. There is a shrine in the back wall of the well-shaft which is approached by a flight of 52 steps. It contains an image of *devi* or mother goddess in the yoga *mudra*. The two upper hands of the goddess hold lotuses while elephants are shown sprinkling water on her. The stepwell derives its name from this small shrine dedicated to the goddess Bhavani, consort of Lord Shiva.[2] While the stepwell is in a state of disrepair, one can still see some beautiful carvings—a noticeable one depicts a king seated on a stool beneath a parasol with two attendants flanking him.

In more recent times, this stepwell has been transformed into a shrine for the mother goddess. There are brightly coloured, garish and gaudy sculptures of the goddess on both sides of the entrance to the stepwell. This provides an interesting example of how modern structures appropriate and reclaim ancient wells and utilise them

[2] Mata Bhavani possesses many of the attributes of the goddess Isis or Cybele.

to serve religious purposes. (See images 11.1, 11.2 and 11.3 in Chapter 11.)

During the regency of Queen Minaldevi, several water buildings were built. The main ones were the Miyanal *sur* at Viramgam, Miyanal *talav* (pond) at Dholka, and the Minal Stepwell at Virpur.

Minal Stepwell

The Minal stepwell in Virpur, near the town of Gondal is also ascribed to Minaldevi. A five-storeyed building, it originally had three pavilion towers and contained beautiful carvings.

Minaldevi is also said to have built Mansar Lake at Viramgam, the irregular shape of which is said to resemble a conch. The surrounding *ghat* or flight of stone steps leading down to the water now contains 357 small temples out of the original 520 (Shastri, 1964, p. 390).

Minaldevi vav or Umreth vav

This stepwll in Umreth, adjacent to the temple of Bhadrakali, is said to have been built by Minaldevi, the mother of Jaisinh Siddharaja in the late eleventh century C.E. It is a seven-storeyed structure and well known for its superb artistic beauty.

Not much is known about the life of Minaldevi except that she was the daughter of Jayakesin of Chandrapur, and the wife of Karnadeva who succeeded his father in 1063–64 C.E. Minaldevi, also referred as Mayanalladevi in some records, was the mother of Siddharaja Jayasimha who ascended the throne in 1093 C.E. Minaldevi served as the regent and ruler during the infancy of her son and carried out the duties assisted by several ministers. For more details on the life of Minaldevi, see Chapter 6.

Kalesvari ni Nal

This stepwell situated in the Panchmahal district is also popularly known as Sasu–Vahu ni vav (mother-in-law–daughter-in law stepwell). Its name may have its origin in the fact that it was commissioned by a mother-in law and daughter-in law. Other scholars are of the opinion that the name is derived from the twin stepwells, one large and the other small, both built in one line. It is located in the Sabarkantha district and belongs to the Solanki period. There are numerous carvings in the stepwells; some are of particular interest such as the one in the northern wall of the larger stepwell which depicts a woman giving birth to a child and the other of the goddess Sitala riding a donkey. The goddess is shown with a broom in one of her four arms. There is also an interesting panel containing the nine planets and the 10 incarnations of Vishnu or Dasavatara. Another unusual depiction is that of a fish (*matsya*) and the tortoise (*kurma*) which are shown on a lotus. These animals, along with the sea monster or *makara* and snakes rarely appear in any other monuments with the exception of water buildings. Their presence in stepwell art is understandable because these creatures live in water and therefore symbolise the life-giving waters.

The second storey of the smaller stepwell attributed to the daughter-in-law contains a sculptural decoration of Sesayin Vishnu, and a panel decoration of the Saptamatrikas or the seven mothers.

This stepwell has yielded some fascinating iconography.

Matri Stepwell, Kankavati

Situated in Dhrangadhra in Surendranagar district, this stepwell gets its name from the goddess Matri, whose image adorns a niche in the lower storey. It is said to have been built by Raja Bhimsinhji and belongs to the Chaulukya period. In addition to the image of Matri, there are shrines dedicated to Matreshwar and Koteshwar Mahadev.

Singer vav

This stepwell built in the name of Singer—the favourite servant or slave woman of Minaldevi, mother of Siddharaj—is located to the east of Kapadvanj. It is now in a state of disrepair. At one time, it must have been an impressive structure. As you descend the steps towards the water, there is an image of the Saptamatrikas in a niche on the left side. On the other side is the image of Lord Ganesha. During the festival of Navratri, the local residents perform and participate in *garba* (folk dances) here.

Utvali Mata ni vav

This stepwell in Dholka was also built by Minaldevi, wife of King Karan and the daughter of King Chandrapur Jaikeshi of Karnataka.

SULTANATE PERIOD

While the origins of stepwells date back to the early period of ancient Indian history, they continued to be built under Muslim rulers. During nearly seven centuries of Muslim rule, a large number of stepwells were constructed under their patronage. They were fortunate to have inherited the artistic legacy from their Hindu predecessors and freely utilised the Hindu artisans and craftsmen to build beautiful stepwells and other monuments. Commenting on its unique qualities, Hope and Fergusson wrote, 'As to style, it was the singular fortune of the Muhammadans to find themselves among a people their equals in conception, their superior in execution and whose tasks had been refined by centuries of cultivation. While molding them, they were molded by them' (Hope and Fergusson, 1866, p. 42). The blending of Hindu architectural styles with the refined and elegant Islamic architectural aesthetic resulted in a distinctive and exquisite form of local architecture in Gujarat, so clearly evident in the various stepwells. The stepwells built under Muslim patronage are devoid of the ornate and extensive representation of human and animals found in Hindu architecture. Instead, they conform to the norms of Islamic architecture by employing geometrical designs and the use of floral patterns.

During the Sultanate period and under Mughal rule (1570–1701 C.E.), stepwells continued to be constructed under the patronage of the rulers as well as by wealthy Hindu citizens. A large number of stepwells built during the Mughal rule were made of brick and mortar. The first storey of the stepwell consisted of a *mandapika*, over which was a dome shaped structure.

While the majority of the architectural works during the Sultanate were religious in nature, there are two exquisite stepwells from the reign of Mahmud Begada that are utilitarian. These are the Bai Harir stepwell and the stepwell at Adalaj, both commissioned by women.

A unique feature of the stepwells built under Muslim patronage was that the figurative art, a defining characteristic of Hindu art was replaced by floral and geometrical designs, in keeping with the artistic conventions and requirements of Islam. However, the Muslim rulers and patrons of art continued to employ Hindu craftsmen and sculptors, which resulted in the inclusion of Hindu and Islamic styles. A good example of this is the Bai Harir stepwell in Ahmedabad which is said to have been modeled on the earlier Hindu stepwell known as the Mata Bhavani stepwell.

Thus, the Muslim invasion of Gujarat did not sound the death knell of Hindu art and architecture. On the contrary, the creative instinct survived the Muslim onslaught and the result was something that was elegant, refined and unique.

Another distinctive charactertistic of these structures was the utilisation of existing materials. This is evident in the stepwell of Adalaj which reused the relief of chains and pot with a flower motif at the top.

The earliest extant stepwell built during the Sultanate period dates from the twelfth century and is located in Bhadresvar, in Kutch district.

Sodhi vav

This stepwell is said to have been built in 1319 C.E. by Sodhi, a woman of the Modh Vanik (merchant) caste during the rule of Raja Mahipal in Junagadh district.

Jethani ni vav

This stepwell in Ghumli must have been at one time an imposing structure, though little of it remains today. It is called 'jethani' which refers to the wife of the elder brother. There are steps leading down to the water and above it are galleries. At the bottom on each side is a niche with beautiful carvings. A particularly striking one is of a cow and a calf eating balls of food. There is also an inscription, fragments of which can still be deciphered. On the basis of this, Burgess conjectured that this stepwell was probably built in circa 1326–27 by royalty (Burgess, 1874–75, p. 182).

Just outside this building is another stepwell—Derani ni vav, a less imposing building, in a state of decay. 'Derani' is a term used for the younger brother's wife.

Yamuna vav

There is a stepwell in Somnath Patan containing an inscription in Sanskrit dated 1385 C.E. It refers to the construction of a stepwell, pond and other water structures by Yamuna, the daughter of the Yadava king Bhima and his queen Manikyadevi in Prabhas Patan (Shelat, 2007, p. 14). The opening paragraph of the inscription also provides details of the construction of the Sangameshwar temple.

Hani vav

This stepwell in Dhandusar in Junagadh is named after Hani. It is said that the stepwell was built by Hani, a young princess of Vanthali in the year 1389 C.E. According to the Sanskrit inscription, Hani was the wife of Vaijyanath, son of Gadadhar, minister of Raja Mokalsinh, the Chudasma ruler of Vanthali during the time when Gujarat was under the sovereignty of Ghiasuddin Tughlak (Shastri, 1964, p. 18). Legend states that mothers who are unable to nurse kept a vow in Hani's name.

Suda vav

This stepwell in Mahuva district of Bhavnagar was commissioned by Saha Jaladevi, the wife of the Suda rulers' minister Vamana. According to the inscription in the vav, it was built in 1380 C.E. for the benefit of the people. The inscription states that Jaladevi and her husband had seven sons. The inscription also mentions a pilgrimage undertaken by one Hiradevi, wife of Satyaraj, the younger brother of king Mahipal (Shelat, 2007, p. 64).

Badula vav

Once the highway to Somnath passed through Mangrol. In the village of Badula, 16 miles on the road from Mangrol to Somnath, is a stepwell which was built in 1384 C.E. under the patronage of two Nagar Brahmin girls to honour their local deity, the mother goddess, and for the comfort of travellers. According to the inscription in the vav, their names were Hansu and Jansu and they were the daughters of the Nagar minister Dhandam and his wife Kilhanadevi. Dhandam may have been the minister to the ruler of Somnath. The inscription informs us that the two sisters were beautiful, talented and accomplished in dance and music. They donated funds for the construction of this vav. This inscription is now in the Junagadh collection (Mehta, 1973, pp. 71–72).[3]

Dholka ni vav

This was built in 1410 C.E. According to the inscription found at the entrance of the stepwell, it was built by Virvansh Sahadev and his wife Sadhu. This stepwell has 17 lines of inscriptions in both Sanskrit and Devanagari (Shastri, 1964, pp. 85–86). It can be inferred from the inscription that Sahadev was an official of the Dholka government and was a trusted official of the king, Sultan Muzzafar Shah. He is

---

[3] The inscription in the Junagadh collection is presently in the Watson Museum in Rajkot.

said to have had two wives both of whom became *satis* after his death. The inscription states that Sahadev's son, Ashachandra, was also cultured like his father. Grief-stricken by the untimely death of their son, the stepwell was built by the parents to honour and bless him. During this time it was not uncommon for men of means to have two or three wives, nor for wives to perform *sati* or self-immolation on the funeral pyre of their deceased husband. The inscription goes on to eulogise the devoted wives who accompany their husbands in death, comparing this brave and selfless act to 'climbing the ladder to heaven' (ibid., p. 86; Shastri, 1991, pp. 77–80).

Halvad ni vav

There are several ancient stepwells in the village of Halvad; popular lore puts these at 999. One of these stepwells is a seven-storeyed structure on which is inscribed the genealogy of Dhrangadhra's Jhala king. In it there is a reference to the king along with his mother, wife or daughter.

The inscription provides the date of 1448 C.E. and attributes the building of the stepwell to Kalyande, mother of the Jhala king Mansinh. According to the inscription, she was the daughter of the Vaghela king Sarangdé and his wife Virade. The inscription in the Halvad ni vav goes on to state that the stepwell was constructed for the benefit of all.

Jhinjuwada ni vav

This stepwell was built in 1481 C.E. in Suryapur, near Wadhwan by the great grandson of a wealthy merchant named Kalhan and his wife.

Veena Vapi vav

This stepwell in Wadhwan, situated between the villages of Rampura and Ratba, contains a stepwell which has four inscriptions dating to 1482 C.E. According to the inscriptions, in the reign of Mahmud

Begada, during the rule of Jhala King Rana Vaghji, a resident of Jhinjuvada, Sheth Veena of the Srimala caste and his two wives Ranibai and Valhadé commissioned the well for the welfare of the people (Shastri, 1964).

Randal vav

This stepwell in the Sabarkantha district in Prantij was dedicated to the goddess Randal whose image is carved in the stepwell. It is said to have been constructed by Raja Bhakarsinh in the fifteenth century. The stepwell has two storeys and has many sculptures and carvings. On one of the niches near the steps, there is an image of Randal Mata and numerous carvings of gods and goddesses on the pillars. On one of these can be found the letters 'Atarmatak', perhaps a reference to some local goddess. In later times, many temples and shrines built around the stepwell were dedicated to Maha Kali.

Bhoj ni vav

This stepwell in the village of Bhoj, built of brick and stone, appears to have been commissioned and financed by the mother and daughters of Sheth Sanga in ca. 1498 C.E. during the reign of Sultan Mahmud I Begada. There is an inscription in Sanskrit and Devnagari script which mentions Sanga and her daughters, Samari, Dhumdi, Hema and Dhemi who provided the funds for the construction of the stepwell. (It appears that the stepwell was built by a Sheth Aja, his brother Kajraj and their nephews.) The inscription in the stepwell pays homage to lord Ganapati, the goddess Sarasvati and Brahma, the creator, and praises its builders. It describes the various structural aspects of the building and mentions the sweet waters of the well, the blue and golden lotus flowers, and the aquatic creatures that delight in its waters. It mentions the joyful cacophony of these aquatic creatures. The inscription states that in the waters reside the images of lords Brahma and Vishnu and that the stepwell was built for the happiness of all four-legged animals (Mehta and Kantawala,1962, p. 196).

Adalaj vav

The Adalaj stepwell, (see images 5.1, 5.2 and 5.3) about 13 kilometres north of Ahmedabad, was constructed by the 'good queen Rudabai' (Inscription at Adalaj in Commissariat,1938, p. 24), wife of Raja Virsimha in the reign of Sultan Mahmud Begada and is one of the finest examples of the fusion of Hindu–Muslim architectural styles. It was built in 1499 C.E. and is square shaped with the well in the centre. It is 250 feet in length and is surrounded by columns on all four sides. The stepwell comprises seven storeys and has three entrances (classified as 'Jaya' vav). There is an inscription of 27 lines in Sanskrit and Devanagari script which states that it was built by Queen Rudabai, queen of Virasimha, the Vaghela ruler, when Mahmud Padshah was Sultan. The inscription goes on to state that the queen 'caused this well to be made, which is like the heavenly river Ganges' (Ibid., pp. 242–43). The inscription is full of praise for the Queen and compares her to Sita, the heroine of the epic Ramayana. It states that Rudabai used 5 lakh tanka from her own treasury to build this stepwell. It praises the stepwell, comparing it to the heavenly Ganges and Mount Kailash. The poet says that the stepwell convinces all of this illusion.

Image 5.1: Women descending the steps to the water at Adalaj

Image 5.2: A view of Adalaj landing platforms and pillars

Image 5.3: View of the ornately decorated walls at Adalaj

There is a love story associated with this stepwell according to which the vav was begun by Rajavirsinh who was killed in battle with Mahmud Begada. The latter became infatuated with the beautiful queen Rudabai and proposed marriage. Grief-stricken, the widow agreed on the condition that the Sultan complete the construction of the well. When the stepwell was near completion, the Sultan once again asked her to marry him. She, however, committed suicide by drowning in the vav and the heartbroken Sultan stopped the construction of the well (Kadikar, 2000, p. 58).

The sculptures and figurative carving on the walls and pillars of the stepwell depict the nine planets, beautiful representations of *devi*, the mother goddess, kumbha (clay pitcher), tiger and elephant engaged in fighting, celestial dancers, Varaha, Kartikeya, Hanuman the monkey god and numerous animals. Below the balconies, there are relief carvings of elephants, etc. In the storey just above the water level, one can see a king sitting on a stool under an umbrella flanked by two attendants; a scene depicting the churning of buttermilk; musicians and dancers; and couples in erotic poses. Objects of ordinary daily life are also depicted like a bed, pitcher, etc.

Dada Harir ni vav or Bai Harir Stepwell

Bai Harir's stepwell (see image 5.4) near the ancient well of Mata Bhavani is located in the suburb of Asarva in the north-eastern part of Ahmedabad. It represents one of the finest examples of architecture from the Muslim period in Gujarat. It is 251 feet long, 16 feet wide, and 32 feet deep. The stepwell comprises a domed pavilion which is distinctly Islamic, adjacent to it is a mosque and fruit orchard.

This stepwell was built in the reign of Mahmud Begada (1453–1511 C.E.) and was paid for by Sri Bai Harir Sultan, the lady superintendent of the sultan's *zenana* or harem. There are two inscriptions in the stepwell—one in Sanskrit dated 1499 and the other in Arabic dated 1500 C.E. The inscriptions provide a wealth of historical and other information, though some of it is contradictory and also controversial. The substance of the inscription says, 'Bai Harir caused a well to be built in Gurjara country, in the village of Harirpur, north-east of Ahmadabad at a cost of 3,29,000 (mahmudis).'

Image 5.4: Dada Harir stepwell showing water channels

The translation reads thus:

(Line 1):   Obeisance to the Creator!
(Verse 1): Obeisance to thee, the lord of the waters, who hast the form of all water!
(Verse 2): Victorius is the mother of the three worlds, the supreme Sakti, Kundalini by name, whose feet are praised by gods and men [and] who ever [exists] in the form of wells.
(Line 6):   makes a reference to the location, time and patron of the stepwell: 'Hail Prosperity! In the Gurjara country, in the glorious city of Ahmadabad, in the victorious reign of the Padshah, the thrice glorious Mahmud—the general superintendent of the door of the King's harem, Bai Sri-Harir by name, caused a well to be built, in order to please God.'

The inscription goes on to state:

'for the use of the eighty four lakhs of the various living beings, who may have come from the four quarters, and are tormented with thirst.'

Line 14 goes on to say 'if one looks at the mass of the deep, nectar-like water [of this well], it seems as though the ocean of milk had taken up its abode in it.'

Line 15 continues, 'as long as the moon and the sun [endure], may this [well] remain for the nourishment of insects, birds, plants and animals!' (Abbott, 1896; Jain-Neubauer, 1981).

Bai Harir is also said to have built the town of Harirpur in a suburb of Ahmedabad. Located to the west of the stepwell is a domed mosque and a mausoleum that still bear her name.

The identity of Bai Harir nevertheless continues to be a subject of considerable controversy. Verses 1 and 2 of the above-mentioned Sanskrit inscription contributes to some of the confusion when it states:

> This well was built by the powerful, religious, chief councilor of the King Mahmud, Harir by name, at the place where four roads meet, crowded with good men who come from the hour quarters. As long as the moon and sun [endure), may [the water of] this sweet well be drunk by men!

Briggs gives us a fascinating account of his travels across Gujarat and Saurashtra in which he makes a mention of this stepwell (1849, pp. 217–19). He also narrates a legend commonly prevalent at the time regarding its builder (see Chapter 6). Brigg's account of the stepwell refers to the northerly inscription, which is in Arabic and in white marble: 'Dada Harir originally established a 'pura' in the vicinity of the bauri [stepwell] and within the bounds of the village of Asarva, and which he called Haripura' (ibid., p. 218). As he notes, this piece of information upsets or at least makes one question the fabulous tale of the nurse.

This stepwell, modelled after the earlier Bhavani stepwell, is one of the finest examples of Muslim architecture. Because of the Islamic influences and patronage it is totally devoid of any human figural representations. Instead, ornamental and sculptural decorations utilise animal motifs with an abundance of geese, peacocks, elephants, horses, lions and floral patterns and highly stylised scrollwork. Despite the fact that this stepwell conforms to the dictates of Islamic architecture, it is a beautiful example of the intermingling and intersection of two traditions, Islamic and Hindu. The stepwell consists of five storeys and each pavilion is 480 metres broad. The pavilion at the entrance of the stepwell *mukha* has a dome above it.

Of particular interest in the sculptural decorations are the tree of life, *Kalpavriksha* (an ancient symbol), lotus rosette in vase, two peacocks which flank the stem of a slender tree and two snakes entwined around the stem of a plant.

The Sanskrit inscription informs us of the names of the *sutradhara*s or the craftsmen, mentioning 'Deva', 'Vira', 'Sri-Girana', 'Sayaa'—all of which are Hindu names. This clearly suggests that the Muslim patrons employed Hindu craftsmen and supervisors in the construction of the stepwell.

Rajbai ni vav or Kherali vav

In Kherali village, 4 miles east of Wadhwan, there is a stepwell with an inscription in Sanskrit–Devnagari dated 1463 C.E. It is said that the stepwell was built by the Parmar ruler Jagdev's minister Lakhdeer Sinh in honour of his wife. The inscription names her as Vejaldevi. The stepwell has seven storeys, 108 steps and is 110 feet deep. On the first floor are niches on both sides which contain images of Matri and Chamunda Mata.

Asapuri vav

This stepwell is located on the southern outskirts of Ahmedabad and is dedicated to the mother goddess Asapuri.[4] According to popular tradition, the stepwell was constructed by Vanjara Asabhil

---

[4] Ashapur or Asapuri is worshipped as the goddess of hope. The earliest mention of her is in the text *Harivamsa* in circa 135 C.E.

probably in the sixteenth century. There is an inscription on a pillar on the second floor on the basis of which some scholars believe that this vav was constructed in 1520 C.E. The stepwell is no longer in use but has become the focal point of the worship of *devi* or mother goddess. The sun, moon and animal figures are depicted on it. Today, the stepwell is filled with garbage and is home to pigeons, squirrels and bats.

Roho ni vav

This stepwell of white marble was built in 1560 C.E. by Raja Shree Nanji's wife Champabai and her daughter Sajjabai and it cost them Rs 51,000. It is located in the town of Palanpur in Banaskantha district. The stepwell has four short inscriptions on its pillars. An image found in one of the two ruined shrines gives the name of Champabai (Valand, 2000, p. 19).

Chamunda Mata ni vav

This stepwell facing the Arabian Sea is located on the banks of the Purna river in Surat district and is named after the goddess Chamunda, one of the many forms of Durga. According to popular legend, in the old days the trident of the goddess travelled across the ocean and back.

MODERN PERIOD

Veshya ni vav

This stepwell constructed between the sixteenth and nineteenth centuries in Limbodra, in the Mehsana district, is also referred to as Modheri Mata ni vav as it is dedicated to the family goddess of the Modh (merchant) community. There is some speculation regarding the name of the vav for the term 'Veshya' refers to a sex worker. Could it have been commissioned by a wealthy sex worker?

Mehsana vav

This stepwell was constructed during the reign of the Mughal Emperor Aurangzeb and contains an inscription in Persian and Sanskrit dated 1674 C.E. According to it, the stepwell was commissioned by Shah Gokaldasa of the Srimali caste and Laghu Sakha and her mother Manabai for the welfare of the people (Shelat, 2011, p. 55).

Shikottari Mata ni vav

This stepwell in Kheda district is dedicated to the goddess after whom it is named. There is an inscription which provides the date of 1698 C.E. It mentions that Nagar Ramaji built this 'vapi' to be used by the people of the town of Petapadraka, modern day Petlad (ibid.).

Gangad ni vav

This stepwell in the Dholka region was constructed in 1706 C.E. According to the inscription found in the stepwell, it was built during the reign of King Sesmalla, the Vaghela king, and is attributed to Goranji, his mother.[5] The inscription says, 'Whoever rules this earth, be they king or citizens protect this vav, and remain healthy, prosperous and receive blessing[s]' (Bhatt, 1914, pp. 191–93). It goes on to state that the stepwell was built to attain fame, benefit families, cows, priests, holy men, to remove obstacles and let the builder attain *moksha*. The Sanskrit inscription begins with an invocation of Krishna, Ganesha, Rudra, and the goddess 'Budh', a popular local female deity. The inscription compares the waters of the stepwell to nectar (Acharya, 1933–35, p. 124). Goranji, who commissioned the stepwell, is referred to as famous and a 'provider of food.' She was the wife of Pruthvi Raja and the daughter of Jambuccha Veraji and Angaraji.

---

[5] The Vaghelas were hereditary lords of the region of Vaghel and also of Dholka.

Laduba ni vav

This stepwell at Khadoli near Jhaghadia in Bharuch district of Gujarat was constructed under the patronage of Laduba, the wife of Rayasimhaji (1764–68 C.E.), the ruler of Rajpipla (Mehta and Jani, 1961). The stepwell contains a bilingual inscription in Sanskrit and Gujarati which contains valuable information about Queen Laduba. This beautiful eulogy of Laduba or Lalkumwar calls her the 'illustrious and clever wife of Rajasimha'. Line six states, 'This pure and steady stepwell with nectar-like water is created in an arid region with new bricks. Sri Laduba's residence in the heaven will last for a period till these bricks last' (ibid... p. 33). Line seven of the inscription praises her piety and states, 'By her this sacred stepwell full of pure water is also constructed for the satisfaction of [the] human beings as well as the herds of animals' (ibid.). According to the inscription, the stepwell was completed in 1782 C.E. and cost Rs 13,000.

Kesarasar ni vav

In the vicinity of Lopiya village in Bhuj, there is a vav which provided water to the local people and travelers. According to legend, in the early 20th century, Kesarbai, a Saraswat Brahmin, and her daughter were inspired by a saint Bhanji Bhagat to use their wealth to build two ponds. Each year on the auspicious day of Bhim Agyarash, the entire village gathered to clean and repair the lake, removing the debris and dirt. This was followed by a communal meal. There is an inscription which provides the date of Samvat 1851 (circa 1795 C.E.). Sadly, the pond is now neglected and the images of Kesarbai and her daughter and the inscriptions are broken and in disrepair.

Sitala Mata ni vav

This stepwell is dedicated to the goddess Sitala who is invoked to cure small pox. The goddess Sitala is the deity who presides over this disease and is worshipped in the villages for protection. Several stepwells are linked to folk medicine. Their waters are said to cure many ailments from earache and fever to barrenness and the inability to produce breast milk.

Ambamata ni vav

In Vadodara's Pratapnagar locality, a small ordinary stepwell in Shakti Krupa society contains a shrine to the mother goddess Ambamata. There are other images in this vav, one of which is the panel containing four standing *devis* (Pathak, 1997, p. 215).

Fuli vav

On the outskirts of the village of Adesar is a stepwell known to the locals as Fuli vav. There is an inscription in the stepwell which recounts the courage and patriotism of the queen. It states that once the stepwell was outside the fort. The ruler of Kutch invaded Adesar when its ruler was out of town. His queen immediately began preparations to defend her kingdom and, with the help of her subjects, built a fortress around the well within one single night to ensure that the enemy would not be able to obtain water from it. The intelligence and courage of the queen forced the Kutch invader to retreat. This account is narrated in the inscription.

It can be inferred from the inscription that in the beginning this stepwell was known as 'Rangvav'; later it was referred to as Fuli vav. It is possible it gets its name from the word *ful* or flower because its waters may have been used for the flower garden. One can see in the stepwell sculptures of ascetics, animals, birds, wrestlers and water carriers (Goswami, 2005, p. 194).

Jiji Bai Rani ni vav

Located near the village of Isanpur, on the outskirts of Ahmedabad, this stepwell is named after a queen called Jijibai (Rawal, 1973, p. 62).

Sati ni vav

In the village of Than in Choteela *taluka* of Surendranagar district, there is a stepwell known as Sati ni vav, built for some pious and chaste widow. According to Vyutpati Shastra, the word *than* is derived from the Sanskrit word *stan* (breast), suggesting that the woman's breast overflowed with milk.

Khodiyar Mata ni vav

This stepwell which is 135 feet long and 40 feet deep is located in the village of Isanpur, on the outskirts of Ahmedabad, and is dedicated to the mother goddess Khodiyar. While the original stepwell had been sealed off, a beautiful engraving is still visible on one of the walls depicting two *hansa* (swans) and a sculpture of Naga, the serpent king. Adjacent to the well is an ornate and brightly coloured temple with numerous representations of Khodiyar Mata which is still in use by the local people.

END OF STEPWELL CONSTRUCTION

The construction of stepwells ended with the establishment of British rule over India and the introduction of taps, tubewells and waterpumps. The last stepwell was built in 1935 on the grounds of the Wankaner Palace. This three-storeyed stepwell consists of subterranean rooms built of marble which contain numerous sculptures and a fountain.

While the ancient stepwells no longer serve their original purpose of providing water for daily use, they have recently become popular locations to shoot films.[6] The air of mystery and romance surrounding the stepwells has survived into modern times.

---

[6] An example of this is a film called *Vanjari Vav* produced several years ago by Mahesh and Naresh Kanodia.

6

Place of Women in Society

Numismatic and epigraphic evidence provide only limited information about the status of women and their place in society. The inscriptions found in the stepwells in Sanskrit, Gujarati, Arabic and Devanagari give us a glimpse of the women who commissioned these stepwells. They provide a unique opportunity to learn more about these women, their names, aspirations, achievements, sacrifices and their wealth. Names like Udayamati, Minaldevi, Bhamadevi, Puri, Rudabai, Rudi, Hansu, Jasu, Bai Harir, Hani, Singer, Leeladevi, Minalde, Premalde, Neenade, Kalyande, Veerde, Samari, Dhumdi, Hema and Dhemi are immortalised in the pages of history. The eulogies praise their beauty and acknowledge their sacrifices as wives, mothers and *sati*s. They compare them to Sita and Lakshmi and, as in the case of Rani Rudabai, credit her for bringing glory to her own and her husband's lineage.

The inscriptions tell us about the devotion and piety of some of these women, while others tell us about servant girls like Adi and Kadi, or Singer, the valued slave woman of Minaldevi in whose name the Queen commissioned a stepwell. Still more unique is the reference to the sisters Hansu and Jasu. The inscriptions in Badula vav praise them for their accomplishments in dance and music and state that they donated money for the construction of a stepwell to honour their mother goddess. However, due to the paucity of available historic written sources, we need to also rely on other sources—such as literary works and the evidence obtained from art and sculpture. It is necessary to state that any conclusions derived from these can only be tentative and hypothetical.

While there are hundreds of grants issues by the kings of Gujarat, they reveal little information other than the names and genealogies of the queens and other royal women. From the inscriptions in the stepwells, however, it is clear that royal women as well as other women of means—from wealthy merchant families and occasionally even servants and courtesans—commissioned stepwells to gain merit and immortality.

INSTITUTION OF MARRIAGE

From the available evidence, it appears that women enjoyed relatively greater freedom and independence in regard to marriage until the seventh or eighth centuries C.E. After this, greater constraints were placed on their freedom. In accordance with the Laws of Manu, women were educated to become good wives and mothers. They did not generally have access to formal Vedic education. However, women, particularly daughters of the royal families, may have had access to education at home and received instructions from learned priests. Literary texts contain several such examples of princesses who were instructed in the ancient *shastras*. Merutunga, the author of *Prabandha Cintamani*, cites the example of the daughter of King Vikramaditya in the city of Avanti who was learned in the *shastra*s (1982, p. 5).

Among the higher castes, widow remarriage was not favoured but there seems to be no absolute ban. The literary sources inform us that the renowned ministers Vastupal and Tejpal were sons of Kumardevi, a widow who had remarried (Shastri, 1964, p. 238). There are other references to widow remarriage in literary sources. Divorce was also not unknown during the period.

Polygamy was not only permitted but also quite prevalent among the nobility. There are several references to co-wives in the available sources.[1] The institution of courtesans was also quite common, especially among the royalty. Merutunga mentions them and refers to a courtesan named Bakula in the harem of King Bhimdev I. King Karna, the Solanki King according to literary sources, was also said to be infatuated with a dancing girl and was ultimately tricked into marrying Minaldevi (ibid., p. 239). According to Merutunga, courtesans were given as gifts and also as payment of a fine to the victor at the end of a battle. He goes on to state that, Bhimdev I sent a courtesan to the court of Bhojraj, along with a learned scholar. Another king gifted a hundred courtesans to the victorious ruler (ibid.). The institution of temple prostitution was also widely prevalent.

The institution of *sati*, the immolation of the widow on the funeral pyre of her husband, while commonly practised among the noble families in northern India, did not seem to exist in Gujarat during the Maitraka period (c.470–788 C.E.). According to Shastri (2000, p. 184), no known sources refer to this institution during the Maitraka period. We have, however, references to women becoming *sati* in the stepwell inscriptions from a later period. An inscription found in Sadadi refers to a pious Jain lady who commissioned a well in honour of her deceased son Tarachandra and his 11 wives who became *satis* upon his death (Forbes, 1924, p. 546). This provides evidence of the practice of *sati* but also testifies to the fact that men of means often had several wives. The inscription found in the stepwells at Dholka also refer to *sati*. It states that for a woman to accompany her husband in death was tantamount to 'climbing the ladder of heaven' (Shastri, 1964, p. 86).

Shastri also mentions certain edicts of Gujarat such as the eulogy of King Dadda III (2000, p.187), which contain reference to the veiling (*avagunthana*) of women. The eulogy of King Dhruvasena

---

[1] An example of this comes from the inscription in the Dholka ni vav. See Chapter 5 for more details.

III and King Siladitya VI allude to the toilet cosmetics of women and the painting of faces (ibid., p. 188). There are references to both divorce and separation as well as the prevalence of slavery where women could be bought and sold.

Despite claims to the contrary, the standards of morality among the higher caste women were far from strict. Ancient texts like *Prabandha Chintamani* and *Rajtarangini* mention the lax morals of the aristocratic women (Shastri, 2005, p. 340). Hemchandra, in his description of King Siddharaja's mother Minaldevi, states that she was forced to give up drinking alcohol during her pregnancy (ibid., p. 354). This suggests that women like men were known to enjoy drinking.

Based on available documents and epigraphic evidence, it seems that during the Chaulukya period, society was gradually becoming more narrow minded and restrictive and this must have had a direct impact on women's lives. While the Chaulukya period saw the construction of many vavs, there is little evidence in them regarding the condition or status of women during that age. It is difficult to obtain accurate information about the position of women in society on the basis of available documents and inscriptions. Despite the greater constraints on their freedom, individual women managed to participate in the public realm. Notable among these was Queen Minaldevi who played a significant role as regent in the infancy of her son Siddharaja. Anupamadevi, the wife of King Tejpal, was also consulted on matters of the state. Because of her sharp intellect and generosity, a large number of religious buildings and institutions were established in Gujarat. However, such women were the exceptions. The majority of women spent their entire lives cloistered behind the four walls of their homes. While women enjoyed few rights in society, they did enjoy certain rights and freedoms in matters of religion and worship. They could go on pilgrimages and widows could remarry. Literary accounts from this age reveal that the practice of polygamy as well as Devdasis was prevalent.

WOMEN'S CLOTHING AND ORNAMENTS

The portrayal of women in stepwell art provides a wealth of information about the garments and the jewellery worn by the women, especially during the Chaulukya period. Women, especially of the upper classes, wore two garments besides a bodice to cover their breasts. The upper garment resembling the present day *odhani* covered the breasts, waist, back and the head while the lower garment comprised a fine cloth tied around the waist. Women enhanced their beauty with various ornaments—waist girdles, bracelets and bangles on the arms and wrists, anklets or *kalla* necklaces, huge *kundala*s in their ears and the *chandla* (*tikka*) on their foreheads (Sankalia, 1941, p. 118).

While the inscriptions in the stepwells do not reveal many details about the lives of the women, we can reconstruct and piece together some information about a few of these women patrons from historical sources, legendary material, popular folklore, art and sculpture.

BIOGRAPHIES OF PROMINENT WOMEN PATRONS OF STEPWELLS

Rani Udayamati

Udayamati, who is said to have commissioned the Queen's stepwell at Patan was the wife/queen of Bhimdev (1022–64 C.E.), and the daughter of Sorath's Chudasma ruler, Raja Khangar. She was one of the two wives of King Bhimdev; the other wife was a prostitute named Bakuladevi whose beauty and charms had captivated the heart of the ruler and who subsequently gave birth to Kshemaraja or Haripala. It was, however, Udayamati's son Karna Bhimadeva who ascended the throne and ruled for 43 years. According to the historical sources, Queen Udayamati served as a regent for her minor son and possessed both wisdom and political acumen.

According to the *Prabandha Chintamani* (Merutunga, 1982), the stepwell at Patan was built under the auspices of Udayamati who was a highly accomplished, cultured and devout queen, as evident from the elegance and artistic sophistication of the stepwell. The sculptural decoration and beauty of this structure is comparable to that of the sun temple at Modhera and the Adinath temple at Mount Abu. During the restoration of the stepwell in the 1980s, a beautiful stone image of Queen Udayamati was discovered which reinforces her claim to being the person responsible for commissioning this majestic stepwell, unparalled in its beauty and splendour.

There are exquisite representations of goddesses or *devi*s in this stepwell. The goddesses include Lakshmi, Parvati, Sarasvati, Uma, Chamunda, Durga, Mahishasura Mardini, etc.

In addition to the depiction of the various goddesses, the stepwell at Patan contains a large number of carvings of *apsara*s that are breathtakingly beautiful. These *apsara*s are portrayed as engaged in various arts—especially dance and music—as well as the daily acts from bathing to enhancing their beauty by applying lipstick and *kohl* in their eyes. These maidens are unselfconscious and fully aware of their beauty and charms. They exude sexuality and self-confidence. Scholars have suggested that such a representation of the female form can be interpreted as indicative of her honoured status in society, for women are depicted in all their facets—wife, mother, lover, goddess, dancer, musician and courtesan. We encounter here not just the seductive lover and the sublime goddess, but also the independent woman.

Minaldevi (Maynalldevi)

Minaldevi was the daughter of the ruler of Chandrapur in the Deccan by the name of Jaikeshi. According to legend, she was determined to marry a person she chose, one who was endowed with beauty, education and courage. She had collected information on all the eligible rulers from different regions and lands. Of all the kings, she was captivated by Raja Karnadeva the ruler of Gujarat, and she resolved to marry none other than him. Having sought her father's consent, the shrewd princess devised a clever strategy to achieve her goal. She sent one of her emissaries disguised as an artist to the court of Karna. When he arrived at his court, he bowed to the King and respectfully said, 'Your Highness, your fame has spread in the four corners of the land. One hears your praises from each and every individual. Thousands of people desire to see you. This humble servant has also harbored the dream of meeting you. I am grateful to God for fulfilling my wish' (quoted in Pandit, 1982, p. 42; also see Forbes, 1924, pp. 105–09). Saying this he presented the King with a beautiful painting, which depicted the goddess Lakshmi dancing in front of a king. In the corner of the painting was depicted a young maiden whose beauty surpassed that of the goddess. Enchanted by the beauty of the young girl, the king inquired about the identity of the woman. The artist informed the King that the young maiden in the painting was Minaldevi, the daughter of Jaikeshi, the ruler of Chandrapur. He went on to say that the King had provided his daughter with the best education and culture and countless kings and princes desired her hand in marriage, but she refused to accept their offers.

King Karnadeva agreed to receive her and Minaldevi arrived in Anhilapura where she and the King got married. It is said that her beauty did not match Karnadeva's expectations and he did not show any affection and love towards his bride, and refused to consummate the marriage. Minaldevi had all the comforts of the world, but lacked the love of her husband. Heartbroken, she considered ending her life. The heartbroken and rejected princesss declared her intention to burn herself on a funeral pyre accompanied by her attendants. Only the intercession of Udayamati, Karna's mother prevented this sacrifice when she declared that she too would sacrifice her life if her son did not relent and accept Minaldevi as his lawful wife. Thus, Karna reclutantly consented (Nilkanth, Vol. 2, 1888, p. 171).

The account goes on to state that Raja Karna was infatuated with a beautiful dancer named Namunjala and ordered his ministers to bring her to his harem for a secret rendezvous. Seeing this opportunity, the minister dressed Minaldevi as the dancer and sent her to the King's chamber in the darkness of night. They spent the night together and in the morning before she left, the clever

Minaldevi asked for the King's ring as a symbol of commitment. Mad with love, the King placed his ring on her finger. According to the story, when Karna found out the truth he was not fully convinced until he saw the ring, and from that day on they lived a happy married life. Minaldevi gave birth to Siddharaja Jaisinh in Palanpur.

According to the historical records, Raja Karna died in 1094 when Siddharaja was still a young boy. A struggle for the throne ensued but eventually Siddharaja was declared the rightful heir. For a short duration, Madanlal, the maternal uncle of Karna, served as the regent for the young ruler. But after his murder, Minaldevi assumed all the powers. She exercised regal powers from 1094 to 1143 C.E. By all accounts, she proved to be an astute and capable ruler, appointing trusted ministers and officials while overseeing the general administration of the kingdom.

She also assumed full responsibility for the education of her son. Though he was her only child, Minaldevi made sure that he was neither spoilt nor pampered and ensured that he acquired the right values. As her son grew older, she taught him all the necessary skills essential for a warrior and king, from horse riding and the use of weapons to wrestling and physical prowess. She also narrated to him the ancient history and traditions of Gujarat to instill in him pride in his land of birth and instructed him on the principles of statecraft and polity.

It is said that from the time Siddharaja was 15, Minaldevi would take him on tours to inspect the kingdom so he would observe firsthand the conditions of his subjects. During their travels, wherever they encountered water shortages, she would get ponds, wells and stepwells built for the public. These include the Minalsar pond in Viramgam and the Malav pond in Dholka (Forbes, 1924, p. 107). The Mansarlake or Minalsar in Viramgam has an unusual irregular shape and is said to resemble a conch. Surrounding the *ghat* or flight of steps, which lead down to the water, are 357 small temples (out of the 520 that originally surrounded the lake), which survive today (Shastri, 2005, p. 390).

The result of all this training was that when Siddharaja was of age and became the ruler of Patan, he was praised by all for his just rule.

Minaldevi is also credited with building the stepwell in Nadiad in Kheda district in 1150 C.E.

According to Merutunga, Minaldevi was not just a patron of the arts and architecture but also a pious and devout queen who persuaded her son Jayasimha Siddharaja to remit the taxes imposed on pilgrims at Bahuloda (ibid., p. 64). According to accounts, Minaldevi had gone on a pilgrimage to Somanath. When she arrived in the frontier town of Bahuloda she found to her utter dismay that a tax was levied on all pilgrims by the Anahilavada Kings, compelling many of them to return due to their inability to pay such taxes. Saddened by the plight of the pilgrims, she returned home and threatened to abstain from food until her son ordered the remission of the tax. Siddharaja yielded to his mother's request and Minaldevi travelled to Somanath to worship the god Shiva with much gold and valuable gifts (account in *Bombay Gazetteer*, 1896, p. 172).

As a queen mother and regent, Minaldevi exercised both power and influence. Not only did she champion the cause of Hindu pilgrims but also extended patronage to Jainism and is credited with supporting the Svetambara sect (Shastri, 2005, p. 312).

Forbes narrates a fascinating story about Minaldevi. According to this, she had a pond constructed in Dholka, known as Meenal-talav. On the east side of this pond, there lived a courtesan whose house was an impediment to the symmetry of the pond. Minaldevi offered a generous sum to purchase it but the courtesan declined and refused to relocate. Rather than use force to get her way, Minaldevi showed her sense of fairness and justice and the tank was built retaining the irregular shape. Local tradition and folklore perpetuates this story in the local proverb, 'Would you see justice, visit the Mulav' (Forbes, 1924, p. 108). This account provides evidence of Minaldevi's sense of justice, strong will and strength of character.

Minaldevi has been immortalised in legend and folklore. While some of the claims cannot be verified historically, there can be no dispute that she must have been a major influence in shaping the character and early years of her son. It is said that when Jayasinha Siddharaja was congratulated on his conquest of Malwa, he replied by crediting his mother and lamenting that she did not live long enough to see him attain glory and fame:

> *No woman should bear*
> *A son like me*
> *Whom fate brought the greatest of his cherished wish*
> *Only when his mother was no more.*
>
> – (Singh, 2004, p. 115).

Paying tribute to this remarkable woman, it has been stated that Minaldevi 'combined the capacity for power with the integrity and will to use it rightly' (Hope and Fergusson, 1866, p. 14).

Rudabai

Queen Rudabai is credited with building the stepwell at Adalaj, one of the most beautiful and well preserved stepwells of Gujarat. The love story associated with the stepwell has already been recounted in Chapter 5.

The Adalaj stepwell contains a Sanskrit inscription of 27 lines on the right side of the well, which provides interesting information on Queen Rudabai. Line 8 of the eulogy, makes a reference to Rudabai, wife of King Virsinh and compares her to Rama and the goddess Lakshmi. It goes on to state that the stepwell commissioned by the Queen is analogous to the river Ganges. Line 10 of the inscription refers to the Queen as 'Sati' and goes on to praise the stepwell comparing it to heaven and as the abode of the Gods. The inscription states, 'First among "Satis", the muse of poets, Rudrarani who like Sita brought glory to her own and her husband's lineage by dint of her character.' The eulogy continues to shower praise on the Queen and goes on to state, 'Who among other queens can compare with Rudrarani?' It ends with the statement that 'as long as there

exists the sun and the moon, may there be peace and steadfastness'
(Inscription at Adalaj vav).

Bai Harir

Bai Harir is credited with building a beautiful stepwell during the
reign of Mahmud Begada (1453–1511 C.E.). There is considerable
controversy regarding her identity. There are two inscriptions in the
stepwell, one in Sanskrit dated 1499 and the other in Arabic dated
1500 C.E. The inscriptions mention with gratitude Mahmud Begada
and state that the stepwell was constructed at a cost of Rs 3 lakh.
On the basis of popular legend and Brigg's account of his travels
through Gujarat and Saurashtra, we can surmise that Bai Harir, who
commissioned the stepwell, was a woman named Resham from the
Garasiya community who converted to Islam and came to be known
has Dhyi Harir (Briggs, 1849). Determined to attract the attention
of the Sultan Begada, she gained entry into his harem as a nurse of
one of the royal children. Employing her considerable charms and
amorous intrigue, she caught the attention of the Sultan and gained
his favours. The legend goes on to state that as a superintendent of
the harem, she amassed a vast fortune and possessed two priceless
anklets (ostensibly a gift from the Sultan), one of which she sold to
finance the stepwell.

While the above tale is based on popular legend, there is no
doubt that she was a woman of power, wealth and influence who not
only commissioned the stepwell, but also the adjacent mosque, her
mausoleum and a sprawling garden nearby with fruit trees. While
conforming to the Islamic tradition which prohibits figurative art,
the stepwell nonetheless reflects the blending of the Hindu and
Islamic architectural styles. The inscription in the stepwell pays
homage to the lord of the waters as well as Shakti, the feminine
principle of the Universe.

From the accounts of the lives of individual women, many of
whom were aristocrats from royal families, one can concur with
the statement of two English travellers, 'We behold her in the

swayambhur mandap choosing her favourite knight, or in the marriage hall shining beside him as the goddess of love beside her lord. An honored mother, guiding the realm of her youthful son or in his manhood aiding him with her counsel and winning him to works of mercy and religion' (Hope and Fergusson, 1866, p. 21).

7

Queen's Stepwell (Rani ni vav) – Patan, Gujarat

The Queen's Stepwell or Rani ni vav is the most majestic and impressive of all the stepwells in Gujarat. It represents the pinnacle of stepwell architecture. Built in 1032 A.D. by Queen Udayamati during the rule of the Solanki dynasty, it was said to have been inundated by the waters of the Saraswati river. After nearly nine centuries of oblivion, it was painstakingly excavated and restored in early 1986. It has now been declared a world heritage site by UNESCO. This stepwell built by Udayamati, the wife of Bhimdev I, the Solanki ruler (1022–63 C.E.), is the grandest, most elegant and spectacular of all the stepwells in Gujarat.

According to historical sources, the ancient capital of Anhilwad–Patan was established in 846 C.E. by Vanraj Chawda and served as the political and cultural centre of the Chawda, Solanki and Vaghela dynasties. Patan was the capital of the Capotkata and Chaulukya dynasties and also the early sultans of Gujarat until 1411 C.E. when Ahmedabad was chosen as the new capital. Patan was renowned as a centre of art, learning and scholarship for over 600 years. During the period when the Chaulukyas ruled Gujarat, trade and commerce flourished as never before and ships sailed from and to Cambay (Khambhat) from distant ports, contributing to the prosperity of

Patan. This fabulous wealth from maritime activities was used to promote art and architecture.

Rani ni vav is described in a fourteenth century C.E. text, *Prabandha Chintamani*, by Merutungacarya: 'Queen Udayamati, the daughter of Naravahana Khangara, built this novel stepwell at Patan or Sripattana, which surpasses the glory of the Sahasralinga Sarovara' (quoted in Sadani, 1998, p. 3).[1] According to the text, the stepwell commissioned in 1063 C.E. by Queen Udayamati is said to have taken 20 years to build. Until recently, scholars like Mankodi and others assumed that the stepwell was constructed by Udayamati, as a memorial for her deceased husband. It was, according to them, a testament of a widow's devotion and love for her husband. However, this view has been challenged in recent times by scholars such as Professor Hariprasad Shastri (1964) who argue that the use of the term 'Rajni' in Prabandha Chintamani implies that she was not a widow when she built it. Had it been a memorial, the term 'Rajmata' would have been used (Sadani, 1998, p. 3).

It is believed that the stepwell was completely inundated by the floodwaters of the river Sarasvati. In the 1940s, excavations carried out under the auspices of the Gaikwad State revealed the existence of this ancient stepwell. Large-scale excavations undertaken by the Archaeological Survey of India in 1986 brought to light this magnificent seven-storeyed structure which has since been restored after nearly nine centuries of oblivion. In 1986, during the course of the excavations, a beautiful image of Queen Udayamati was unearthed.

The Queen's stepwell is regarded as the finest example of stepwell architecture in Gujarat and its sculptures are comparable to the Surya Mandir of Modhera and Adinath temple in Mount Abu. According to Commissariat, the date of its construction is 1032 A.D. The style of architecture corresponds to that of the Jain temple of Vimalsha on

---

[1] The Sahasralinga pond built by Udayamati's grandson Siddharaja (1093–1143) was said to contain 1,000 shrines dedicated to Siva and is one of the largest of its kinds in Gujarat.

Mount Abu, which was built the same year (Commissariat, 1938, p. 1). This magnificent stepwell consists of multi-storeyed columnades and walls, which lead up to a deep circular well. Columns, pillars, brackets and beams are rich in ornamentation and scroll work and the niches of the walls are carved with exquisite figures (see Images 7.1 and 7.2). The entrance to the stepwell is on the east and the well is located in the west. According to the classifications of the different types of stepwells provided in the ancient texts, this would belong to the 'Nanda' category. The stepwell is 65 metres long, 20 metres wide and 28 metres deep. There are ornate and exquisite carvings on the walls from the ground up to the sixth storey. The seven storeys of the well are decorated with 'Vanasthali' or a forest of 212 pillars (Sadani, 1998, p. 51).

Over 800 large sculptures decorate the walls of the seven terraces. The construction of the stepwell is strongly reminiscent of the temple of Khajuraho and reveals Brahmanical influence, which represents the classical tradition of Hinduism centred around the worship of the gods Shiva, Vishnu and Brahma.

Image 7.1: Queen's stepwell—A view from the top

Image 7.2: A view of the Patan stepwell wall

The ornate wall (Image 7.3) includes sculptures of Vishnu, Brahma, Shiva and *apsaras* and *devis* (goddesses). Notable among the sculptures are the incarnations of Lord Vishnu, Ardhanarisvara (a representation of the unity of the male and female forms) and a profusion of *apsaras*. A charming depiction is that of an *apsara* who appears to be applying what seems to be lipstick or chewing on an aromatic twig, while a man tickles her foot (see Image 7.4). Another particularly charming depiction is of an *apsara* combing her hair, admiring herself in the mirror and adjusting her ear ornament (see Images 7.5 and 9.1). Included in this panel from the Queen's stepwell is the image of *devi* with multiple arms (see Image 7.5). On the third terrace wall facing north is the depiction of an *apsara* warding off a monkey who clings on to her legs causing her garment to slip down, revealing the sensuous contours of her body (see Image 7.6). At her feet is what appears to be a deformed nude female with a snake around her neck. Mankodi speculates that this may possibly be an erotic motif (See Images 7.6 and 9.1).

Image 7.3: Sculptures adorning the Queen's stepwell, Patan

Image 7.4: Maiden applying lipstick

Image 7.5: A panel from the Queen's stepwell

Image 7.6: Maiden with a monkey climbing up her left leg

There is an exquisite image of an *apsara* with long hair and a swan (the 'Nagakanya' or serpent princess; see Image 10.2 in Chapter 10). The wall carvings also depict graceful dancers in classical dance postures and *Kalpavriksha*, an ancient symbol of a tree depicting fertility and a remnant of nature worship.

At the entrance wall of the stepwell, facing the north are lattice work patterns in stone. These beautiful geometrical patterns and designs bear an uncanny resemblance to the ancient textile tradition of Patan called Patola, which forms a part of the living tradition of Gujarat. The beautiful Patola sarees and textiles are still woven by weavers in Patan and are similar to the designs on the Patan stepwell wall (see Image 7.7).

Image 7.7: Lattice pattern on the stepwell walls

The art of the Queen's stepwell is prodigious and highly ornate. It depicts the entire cosmos inhabited by gods and goddesses, humans, flora and fauna, fish and birds and all kinds of animals, real and mythical. Conforming to the 'great tradition' of Brahmanical Hinduism, the sculptures in the Queen's stepwell depict the Indian pantheon of Brahma, Vishnu and Shiva along with those of Shakti, Ganesha, the 24 forms of Vishnu, his 10 incarnations including Vamana, Rama, Balarama, Buddha and Kalki. While the sculptural images in the Queen's stepwell depict numerous deities, the stepwell reflects the Vaishnava faith of its patron; images of Vishnu abound and outnumber all others. However, what is especially striking is the portrayal of women, not just goddesses who are venerated, but women as objects of adoration.

The figurative art depicts the entire spectrum of the everyday life and activities of women. Among the many images are those of the *nayika* or heroine admiring her beauty in the mirror while she adjusts her ear ornament; the *nayika* writing a letter to her lover; the maiden with a scorpion climbing up her right leg as she unknowingly lets her clothing slide off (Image 7.8). In the right panel of Image 7.8, a maiden is seen pulling the beard of the dwarf-like man infatuated with her loveliness (Sadani, 1998, p. 46). Image 9.2 in Chapter 9 shows a maiden with a fishplate in her hand, threatening the snake which is encircling her leg as if reaching up to grasp at the fish. There is an enchanting figure of a maiden who has just stepped out of the

Image 7.8: Maiden with a scorpion climbing up her right leg

bath, her hair still wet and dripping with a swan at her side trying to catch the drops of water mistaking them for pearls (Image 10.2 in Chapter 10).

Love is a recurring theme—sublime, sensuous, and hinting at eroticism. The graceful women in the sculptures are, however, unselfconscious. Their garments are elegant, their hair perfectly coiffured and their bodies are adorned with jewellery—necklaces, earrings, bangles, anklets and waist girdles, etc. What we witness is a joyful celebration of a woman's body, her loveliness in all its facets. We see here the female as goddess, wife, lover, mother, dancer, musician, queen and ascetic. The art of the stepwell gives full expression to all the *rasa*s or emotions found in Indian aesthetic theories—from love and loneliness, anger and fear to humour and bliss.

Sadani has appropriately referred to the Rani ni vav as an underground shrine. Although dedicated to Lord Vishnu, the numerous Hindu deities along with their families are accorded a place of honour and reverence and the stepwell symbolises religious harmony and tolerance. Of the 800 or more sculptures, we will now examine the notable ones.

Vishnu

As the supreme lord who is the creator and source of the cosmos, Vishnu is the pre-eminent deity in the Queen's stepwell, which is dedicated to him. The images of Vishnu and Parvati outnumber all the other deities in this stepwell. Almost the entire terrace on the third storey is devoted to Vishnu's 10 incarnations. Indian iconography is rich in its depiction of Vishnu reclining on the multi-headed snake, Ananta Naga or Sesa floating on the cosmic waters. These images are described in three ways—Jalasayi, Sesasayi and Anantasayi; the Jalasayi Vishnu is most commonly found in the sculptures and figural representations in reservoirs, wells and stepwells. The association of Vishnu with the cosmic waters from which the universe itself was created, therefore, explains his presence in water architecture, especially in the Rani ni vav. Vishnu is shown reclining on the cosmic waters holding a conch, mace and a lotus flower. From the navel of the Lord, emerges the lotus on which is seated the God Brahma; Lakshmi, the divine consort of Vishnu, is depicted seated at his feet. The goddess Lakshmi is also called Bhudevi, symbolising the earth goddess.

Lakshmi

Some exquisite images of Lakshmi in the Patan stepwell form a part of the mythical theme of the churning of the ocean. The image of Lakshmi in a yogic pose has been compared to the one in Sasu na Dera in Rajasthan from the eleventh century.

Garuda

There are a number of images of Garuda, the eagle, with goddess Lakshmi and Lord Vishnu, the latter seated on Garuda. An arm of Lakshmi encircles and embraces his neck and the other holds a lotus. This sculpture shows beautiful female attendants surrounding the image of Vishnu and Lakshmi with flywhisks in their hands.

Devis or Female Deities

The worship of the mother goddess dates backs to the dawn of Indian history. As early as the Indus Valley Civilisation (2500–1500 B.C.E.), we have evidence of the active worship of the feminine deity in countless clay and terracotta figurines of the mother goddess. Coomaraswamy is of the opinion that they evolved from *yakshinis* or fertility spirits, associated with trees (1995, p. 9).

In the Rani ni vav, there are a large number of images of *devis* or the mother goddesses. From the earliest times in India, the worship of female divinities or mother goddesses constituted an essential part of worship. These goddesses were at the heart of a cult exclusive to women, and in the villages and countryside this continues to flourish today. These local goddesses are worshipped and their blessings invoked by women for the protection, health and well being of their husbands and families.

Among the figural representations of the *devi* and those representing the Shakti sect are numerous ones of Lakshmi, Parvati, Sarasvati, Chamunda, Durga and the Saptamatrikas. There is an image of Mahishasura Mardini (Durga slaying the buffalo headed demon) with 20 arms, as well as images of Brahma–Savitri, Uma–Maheshwar and Lakshmi–Narayana in the north side of the stepwell.

Parvati

There are at least eight representations of the goddess Parvati in the Queen's stepwell. One of the most beautiful depicts Parvati's penance—she is standing on one leg like an ascetic practising penance and austerities amid the four fire altars for the purpose of divine intervention. According to Mankodi, the Queen's stepwell was built to commemorate the death of Udayamati's husband, and the image of Parvati's penance to honour her husband Shiva was equated with Udayamati paying homage to her deceased husband while expressing the desire to be reunited with him. Mankodi convincingly argues that the goddess serves as an archetype for the Queen (1991, p. 235). Excavations at the Queen's stepwell have unearthed at least 15 separate images of Gauri and Parvati.

Durga (as Mahishasura Mardini, the slayer of the demon Mahishasura)

A lovely image of goddess Durga is located in a niche in the western wall of the stepwell. The goddess has three eyes and her prowess is represented by 20 arms (in which she holds numerous weapons like the trident, discus, bow, shield, and also a drum). She is riding a lion, which is her vehicle and her right leg is crushing the demon's back. The lion is shown attacking the demon from the rear while the goddess slays him with her trident (see Image 9.1 in Chapter 9).

Kshemankari Devi

There is an image of Kshemankari devi on the western wall of the second landing with two female attendants on either side of the devi. Kshemankaridevi, also known as Khimaj Mata, is the patron goddess of numerous occupational groups such as carpenters, goldsmiths and tailors, as wells as some Jains.

Uma–Maheshwar

There is an image of the two in the fourth landing of the stepwell. Shiva is depicted with four arms, one of which holds a serpent while the lower arm embraces Uma. On the left hand corner is an *apsara* playing a musical instrument.

Suryani

There is an image of Suryani, the consort of Surya (the Sun God), on the first floor of the stepwell. She has four arms. On both sides of her legs are four female attendants.

Saptamatrikas

The Saptamatrikas or seven mothers are the agents by means of which the cosmos is reborn and renewed. They are symbolic of both life and death, and thereby embody benevolent as well as malevolent forces. Harper, who has written on the seven Hindu goddesses of spiritual transformation, states that the Saptamatrikas occupy a relatively insignificant place in the classical literary texts. They were relegated to a subordinate position to the male deities Shiva and Vishnu. They, however, occupy a prominent place in stepwell art and their images can be seen in Adalaj, Patan's Rani ni vav, Singer vav and Kaleshvari ni Nal. In folk religion, they are linked with human reproduction and fertility as well as cosmic renewal (Harper, 1989). According to Enthoven and Jackson, the seven mothers are identified with the planets that influence the life of the child in the womb. One of these is Randalmata or Rannadevi, the wife of the sun who presides over child birth (Enthoven and Jackson, 1989, p. 72).

In Vedic culture, the number seven was regarded as auspicious and represented wholeness and fulfillment. Harper states that the number seven is associated in folk religion with ideas of purity, pollution, specifically pollution caused by menstruation, and purification (Harper, 1989, p. 27).

Navagraha (or the Nine Planets)

The nine planets consisting of the Sun, Surya, along with Chandra, Bhauma, Buddha, Sukra, Brhaspati, Sani, Rahu and Ketu are worshipped by the Hindus and their images are generally found in Shaiva temples. The ancient poets and philosophers in gazing at the bright planets in the night sky envisioned Vishnu sleeping on the seven-headed serpent embodying eternity. There is a popular belief that the planets were once the great sages who conferred the gift of wisdom on humankind.

Varaha

In the south wall of the stepwell, there is a beautiful image of Varaha. The face is that of a boar with a crown on its forehead and a necklace. The boar has four arms, holding a mace, shell and on his elbow sits the goddess Earth whose left hand is stroking the boar's face. The lower left hand holds a *chakra* or disk (See Image 9.2 in Chapter 9).

Vamana (Dwarf)

The Vamana is one of the many incarnations of Lord Vishnu. The stepwell image of Vamana depicts a short and plump dwarf in a bent position. He has long ears and a one-stringed necklace around his neck. In his left hand is an umbrella.

Kalki

There is a sublime image of Kalki, the last incarnation of Vishnu, in the Patan stepwell. He is depicted riding a horse with a crown on his head, earrings, necklace and boots on his feet. On his left stands a female figure with a pot from which she is pouring wine into the hands of Kalki. Another female figure is using a flywhisk; another figure is shown asleep behind the horse's leg. One can also see sculptures of mother goddesses on the waist band.

Narsinh

On the south wall is a beautiful sculpture of Narsinh, the 16-armed half man and half lion. The image depicts Narsinh's left leg resting on the demon which he dismembers with his two hands.

Sarasvati

Sarasvati is the name given to a mighty river revered along with the Ganges and Yamuna. Sarasvati, the goddess of learning, is depicted in the Patan stepwell along with her vehicle, the swan. The worship of Sarasvati can be traced back to the Rig Vedic age. Initially, she was worshipped in the form of the river of the same name, but with the passing of time she gradually became a symbol of learning, music, speech and art. She is also revered as the patron of lakes, tanks and stepwells.

The goddess Sarasvati, consort of Lord Brahma, the creator, is depicted in stepwell art as the embodiment of knowledge and the arts. She is shown with a book in her hand, indicating knowledge and intelligence, and the musical instrument, the veena, suggesting her role as the goddess of music.[2] One can surmise that in the age when these sculptures were produced, there must have been some learned women who chose to pursue knowledge and who

---

[2] In Hindu and Jain traditions, Sarasvati is depicted with the veena, a lotus, *kamandal* (earthen or metal pot for pouring water) and *akshamala* or a rosary.

were also accomplished in music (see discussion of Badula vav in Chapter 5).

There is a beautiful standing image of Sarasvati on the east side of the third storey of the stepwell. Sarasvati's face has an expression of joy and contentment (Savalia, 1991, p. 74). She is adorned with a jewel-studded crown and wears ornaments on her neck, ears, head and body. The goddess has four arms. The lower right hand is shown to be blessing someone, the upper hand holds a rosary, her upper left hand has a veena while in her lower left hand she has a water pot. There is also an image of Ganesha along with the seven mothers. On the right side of the goddess are seated images of Kaumari and Vaishnavi along with standing images of Varahi and Aindrani. On the left side are a seated Ganesha and Chamunda. Below them are standing images of Brahmi and Maheshwari.

In the Hindu pantheon of gods—especially Trimurti—Brahma occupies an important place, by virtue of being the creator of the Universe and the chief among the deities. He is depicted with one face, a long beard and seated in the Lalitasana. He has four arms, three of which hold a garland, book and water jar while the fourth embraces his consort Savitri.

On the north wall of the fourth storey, there is a beautiful image of Brahma and Savitri. Brahma is seated on a lotus throne with his right leg dangling. In the left leg is the seated image of Savitri. Both are decked in ornaments.

Animal Figures

There are countless representations of animals in stepwell art and they include elephants, lions and horses. They serve the purpose of decorating the pillars and basement mouldings. In the Queen's stepwell as well as at Adalaj, there are rows of horses or *asvathara* and elephants or *gajathara*. The elephants are shown in a playful mood or engaged in fighting.

The animal forms also include representations of mythical animals— through the *kirtimukha* or victory faces.

Mythical Figures

The *kirtimukha*s decorate the doors of shrines, basement and shafts of pillars. The evolution of these mythical figures can be traced back to the temples of the Gupta period; later they became a standard feature of medieval Indian temples.

The *kirtimukha*s translated as the 'face of fame, glory or renown' are found in the *grasapatti*, a moulding with relief carvings of grinning faces with horns. Their origin is given in an account in the Padma Purana, and they represent a decorative form dating back to antiquity. These mythical figures can also be seen in the old temples in Java.

Themes of Maternal Love

There are numerous sculptures in the Queen's stepwell of Matr-Vatsalya, depicting the theme of maternal love and the tenderness towards infants—a recurring and common theme in Indian culture and literature (See Image 7.9). In the words of Sadani, 'it is precisely the human mother who transcends into the divine mother. She not only tames, trains and nurtures man into culture, but all the cultures and civilizations are nurtured in her benevolent laps' (Sadani, 1998, p. 43).

In one of the sculptural images, the woman holds the child in her arms, pointing at the moon to divert its attention. This is reminiscent of poems celebrating and exalting Krishna as the mischievous and irresistible child insistent on wanting the moon. Krishna says, 'mother give me the moon for playing' (Sadani, 1998). Yasoda, his adoring mother epitomises maternal love.

Another image in the Patan stepwell depicts a mother in a mango grove with a child clinging to her waist and another beside her. One can see bunches of mangoes hanging in the background. Still another image depicts a mother raising her child high to allow it to pluck a mango from a tree. The recurrence of the mother–child theme in the sculptures expresses the tender emotions of maternal love and the delight and joy experienced by women in their children. Image 7.9 is a beautiful representation of *vatsalya* or maternal love.

Image 7.9: A woman with an infant

Women are portrayed in the Queen's stepwell in all their facets. In addition to the woman as mother, wife and goddess, she is also frequently shown as the embodiment of sexual love and beauty.

Women's beauty, their seductive charms and their irresistible appeal is graphically depicted in many of the images at Patan. In one such carving, the *nayika* or heroine is shown with a bearded man who is gazing at her, spellbound by her loveliness. He is smaller in stature compared to her. According to Sadani's interpretation, the *nayika*, the object of this adoration, holds the beard of the man while her left hand tries to restrain his advances in an admonishing stance (see the extreme right panel in Image 7.8). The artist here is evoking the *hasya-rasa* or the emotion of humour in the spectator (Sadani, 1998).

Women are portrayed in their beauty in their numerous forms—as goddess, friend, mother, lover or companion. Every facet of their lives, their daily activities are depicted in the art with tenderness and understanding. Could this be an indication of the high regard and respect accorded to women? Does this suggest their high status in society? While it may be difficult to determine women's status in society purely from their depictions in art and sculpture, it would not be incorrect to conclude that women who were single, independent and accomplished were respected in society. Women gained fame and renown for their wit, knowledge, intelligence and accomplishments.

Many of the sculptural images depict the *apsaras*. These lyrical figures are sensuous and elegant and they are shown engaging in various activities. The objective of the artist is to celebrate the beauty of these maidens but equally to arouse in the spectator, his audience, one or more of the *rasas* or emotions, which range from humour to love, repulsion and longing.

Image 7.10 depicts elaborate and ornate figurative sculptures from the stepwell wall. The figure on the extreme left is of an *apsara* in a dance pose. The second image is that of God Ganapati. The third depicts a maiden pouring water from a water pitcher. The fourth depicts a devi (mother goddess).

Image 7.10: Queen's stepwell, Patan

The Queen's stepwell and its opulent art awes and dazzles us with its beauty. As a patron and donor of this stepwell, Udayamati has immortalised herself and secured a unique place in the pages of history.

Describing the sublime art of the Patan stepwell, Sadani has so aptly said, 'As we behold the beauty of [the] Queen's stepwell, we are transported to a realm where eternal beauty floats on the cosmic waters of the well. This grand monument is the sweetest song of Queen Udayamati culminating in cadence of prayers,' (1998, p. 53).

8

Voices from the Deep[1]

WOMEN, FOLKLORE AND WATER

Sanskrit poetry as well as folk literature in India contain numerous descriptions of water architecture and water buildings. These served as the setting for water sports, festivals and celebrations in classical texts such as the *Kama Sutra* and *Karpurmanjari*.[2] The folktales are known as *lok katha* or *lokvarta* and were transmitted orally by professional storytellers or bards known as Bhat, Charan, Barot and Bharthari in Gujarat.

The deity most commonly associated with water sports is Lord Krishna, the divine lover of the Bhagvata Gita. Beautiful descriptions of water games abound in the Bhagvad Purana in which Krishna frolics and flirts with the *gopi*s, the cowherd maidens, while engaged in water sports. This theme also inspired countless paintings. During these festivals, young maidens dressed in orange garments and adorned with jewellery, drink alcohol, sprinkle perfumes on their bodies and participate in water games (Jadav, 1997, p. 50).

The Rasa or Garba, the traditional folk dance of Gujarat

[1] All the folksongs in this chapter are translations from the original Gujarati into English. Many of them are from Gaudani, 1968. I am indebted to Dr Kansara and Ms Sudha Mehta for help in the translations.

[2] *Kama Sutra* is dated approximately first century C.E. *Karpurmanjari*, a drama by Rajasekhara, is said to have been written in circa 900 C.E.

performed at night, narrates tales of Krishna and the *gopi*s. In it
there are frequent references to a water source. One such song
states:

> *The pond is filled with milk,*
> *Its walls are studded with pearls*
> *We had gone to dance the* garba
> *Or celebrate life?*

In Gujarat and Rajasthan, women are responsible for fetching
water. Stepwells and wells represented their space. In the early
hours of the morning and at dusk, gaily dressed women converged
here with their shining brass or copper pitchers balancing on their
heads to draw water. The sound of their anklets and the music of
their laughter and chatter filled the air and this setting became a
favorite subject of poets and folklorists. It was near the lake, pond,
well or stepwell that women expressed their sorrows and their joys
The fetching of water was viewed as a sacred duty and that is the
reason that the pots (*bedu*) are of silver and the load mounting ring
(*endhoni*) is golden and beautifully decorated.

Referring to this theme, one song states:

> *My mounted water-pot is golden, O handsome Samaliya!*[3]
> *My knitted ring supporting the water-pot over the head,*
> *Is studded with jewels, O handsome Samaliya!*

There are countless songs that depict maidens going to the wells
to fetch water and the mischievous pranks performed by Krishna.
The devotional poetry of Surdas and Dayaram also address this
theme. One such example goes:

> Here come the water-pots mounted one upon
> another and brimming with water.
> Here come the damsels joyfully smiling.
> The mounted water-pots of my she-friend

---

[3] Samaliya here refers to Krishna.

Women took great pride in their shining, glistening pots which they scrubbed till they shone like the golden rays of the sun. In a poem a woman expresses her longing for a beautiful water pot:

> *I am not going to draw water from a copper pot,*
> *O Mother,*
> *I yearn for a golden one!*

There are numerous references to wells and ponds in folklore in which the imagery is vivid and beautiful. One of the songs says:

> *We had gone to take up the refrain of the song.*
> *We had gone to dance around the lamp in the pot.*
> *The tall, fair and beautiful damsel goes to fetch water*
> *But the thorn of love has pierced her; her water-pot*
> *Is tottering.*

Lost in the thoughts of her beloved, the maiden stops in the path while her water pot sways to and fro.

Many of the folksongs describe the lovelorn maiden and her feelings and emotions that range from ecstasy and longing to fear and apprehension. Women in the villages of Gujarat walk to the water source with two or three glistening pots piled one on top of the other, supported by a small embroidered or knitted ring on their head. Striding gracefully, her arms free, she provides a beautiful sight that has been the subject of countless popular folk songs:

> *I went, today, to fetch water, O my girl-friend!*
> *And, the loving glances of Dagara put a spell on me!*
> *Alas, my water pot would remain empty,*
> *Even if I fill it repeatedly!*

The echoes of lovers planning to elope are still heard on the banks of rivers and wells. Picture the lovebirds Mithdi of Deha village and her lover Nathio here:

> *'O Mithdi of Deha, look Nathiyo is standing yonder,*
> *What cloth for you should I bring for your blouse O Mithdi,*

What sari would you like?
O Mithdi of Deha, tell me what sari would you like?'
Runs with speed, does run Nathiyo with speed,
Runs Nathio eloping with Mithdi of Deha,
He indeed runs away with speed.

The wells, stepwells and ponds were also popular sites for the women to perform rituals and religious rites. These very often centred around fertility and a woman's yearning for children, a common concern for all women. This emotion was particularly intense in India where women felt fulfilment from becoming a mother of many sons and childlessness was considered a curse. A popular song in the Kheralu area focuses on this theme:

I am coming fast with the water-pot filled with water,
O Rannade![4] Please give me the one who would pull
Me by the skirt
O Mother! The taunts of childlessness are unbearable.[5]

This was a common refrain. Women who were unable to bear children suffered the taunts and humiliation in society and appealed to the mother goddess to bless them with a child. No humiliation was greater than the curse of barrenness.

Another recurring theme in folklore revolves around sacrifice to propitiate the deities and to produce the desired outcome. After a long, hot summer, Indians looked to the skies for the first signs of rain and longed for the monsoons that would irrigate the parched land and bring relief to man and beast, filling the wells, ponds and reservoirs. When the rains failed and water became scarce, the wells remained empty. No sacrifice was seen as too great to quench the thirst of the village and ensure survival. The sacrifice of human life was regarded as necessary for the well being of the community. Many folksongs deal with this theme. The best known is about

[4] Rannadé refers to the wife of the Sun. She is also referred to as Randalmata
[5] A barren woman is contemptuously referred to as *vanjani* in Gujarati.

the Madhavav (see Chapter 5). According to legend, Madhava, a Nagar Brahmin, the minister of King Karan Ghelo, had a stepwell constructed in Wadhavan. The song goes:

> *For twelve long years, we dug a well*
> *But could not locate the underground stream, O My Dear!*
> *Astrologers of fame were summoned who predicted, O My Dear!*
> *The sacrifice of our son and his wife;*
> *We hope, profuse water could be located, then.*
>
> *The couple descended down to the fifth step,*
> *The water in the well flowed and immersed them upto the neck.*
> *As they stepped down to the sixth and seventh step,*
> *The head dress and the silken sari were found floating on the water!*[6]

Thus, according to the legend, the sacrifice by the young couple filled the stepwell with water.

The waters of the wells were perceived as sacred and compared to the river Ganges. Just as a dip in the waters of the Ganges cleanses all sins, so bathing with the waters of the well was viewed as an act of purification. It was also believed to cure many diseases, such as leucoderma. Alluding to this theme, one song states:

> *… when the underground stream flowed with water*
> *The Ganges has arrived ceremoniously to Gangava*[7]
> *Let us go, take bath and make ourselves happy!*
> *White spots would be cured, and we would become golden;*
> *Let us go, take a bath*
> *The revered Ganges has arrived ceremoniously.*

Another folksong popular in the Soratha region in Gujarat appeals to the local goddess to heal the afflicted:

---

[6] The headdress refers to the *paghadi* worn by men, especially in Saurashtra.

[7] Gangava is a bowl-shaped stepwell located in Dehadara, a village about 8 miles from Wadhavan. According to popular belief, the river Ganges manifests every new moon day in the Indian month of Bhadarvo.

We went to the Manasarovara to fetch water, O Generous One of
Dadava!
Some blind ones and lame ones stopped us at the door of the
pavilion;
Please confer eyes to the blind ones,
O Rannade! O Generous One of Dadava!

According to popular lore, it does not matter whether the water has been obtained from a well, stepwell, tank or stream. For a woman it represents the waters of the sacred Ganges and Yamuna rivers. Another poem expresses the same idea thus:

The Ganges and Yamuna rivers are in my water vessel,
I go to the well for water.

Stepwells and wells served as the inspiration for countless songs and poems which describe the emotions and feelings of the young women who went there to get water and the chance encounters and liaisons that resulted. One such song goes:

How can I go to fetch water, O friend of mine
How can I go to fetch water?
A stranger standing at the steps of the well
Made me bashful and lose all control.
How can I go to fetch water, my dear friend?

(Gaudani, 1980, p. 204)

In another song, the young woman who goes to the well comes across ascetics who ask for some water:

Ascetics at the well I found,
To give them water to drink.
Alas! My rope was not long enough,
Tried so much though I did.
Now how shall I quench their thirst?
How could I do without my Hari?[8]

---

[8] 'Hari' is a term used for god.

So I tore my sari and made a rope,
Pushed the pot under water with it,
Found water for the thirsty holy men,
How could I do without my Hari?

There are numerous songs and stories about one Lakha Fulani who is remembered for his love of nature, women and his poetic temperament. One such anecdote narrates Lakha Fulani's aesthetic sense and his eye for beauty. Looking at some beautiful ladies washing their feet at the banks of river Shetrunji and enjoying themselves, Lakho Fulani tells his friends:

Dear friends! Just look!
How they are enjoying themselves at the banks of River Shetrunji?
How lucky are the stone slabs!
These beautiful ladies are washing their clothes with their hands moving so strongly!
And the slabs have now turned so smooth by the constant washing!
They also wash their pinkish heels on the small slabs and make them turn red!
They are so enjoying themselves at this work!
...
Their hands move with such grace
These women at play.
Friends, let my funeral be held on slabs
Smoothened by the touch of their feet.

Another popular folk tale recounts the story of Adadi, a young girl who goes to fetch water. There, she encounters her lover Harisang who has come to get water for his horse. He helps to lift the water-filled pot and place it on Adadi's head. She suggests that they elope and they run away together. On the way, they suffer pangs of hunger and buy some sweets worth half a rupee which they eat on the banks of the pond. Adadi, now thirsty asks for water and her lover digs a hole in the sand. Water flows from it and both of them joyously scoop the water from the ground in the hollow of their palms and drink it.

> *Adadi is going to Sarovar to fetch water*
> *To fetch water indeed;*
> *Harisang came there to give water,*
> *To his horses indeed;*
> *Harisang helps place the pots on her head...*
> *And now she wants water,*
> *She wants water to quench her thirst.*
> *Harisang digs a hole in the sand*
> *And joyously they scoop out water*
> *in the palm of their hands.*

Sometimes a chance encounter near the water leads to love and marriage:

> *Tall cowherd damsel, with garland of golden leaves,*
> *Passes, carrying on her head a pot filled with milk;*
> *She walks along the river,*
> *While Krishna, the cowherd stands on the yonder bank.*
> *Whose daughter are you? Whose wife?*

To this she replies:

> *I am the daughter of Rama, the cowherd man.*
> *I have neither home, nor place,*
> *Nor am I married.*

Krishna sends a proposal to her father asking for her hand in marriage. The tale has a happy ending with the marriage of Krishna and the daughter of Rama, the cowherd.

Many wedding songs are also connected with vavs and water structures. In folklore, the poet imagines that Lord Shiva (Shankar) goes to the water bank to wash his *dhoti* or garment and there he meets Parvati, his future bride:

> *That pond is full of milky water,*
> *And its bank is made up of pearls;*
> *God is washing his* dhoti *and Parvati is pouring water;*
> *Wash your* dhoti *gently, or water would splash on her clothes.*

At home grandfather would be angry and mother would swear at me;
No, no, neither is your grandfather angry, nor would mother swear,
For, both of us shall marry, in this month of Vaishakh. It's my promise.

Another beautiful marriage song draws a fine picture of a stepwell:

Sri Rama, white city, White Dholka,[9] *Oh Beautiful*
Sri Rama, white is the stepwell of dear dholakiya, Oh Beautiful.
Sri Rama, the stepwell has the copper lock, Oh Beautiful.
Sri Rama, the full water is pearl coloured, Oh Beautiful.
Sri Rama, the waste in the stepwell is turmeric red, Oh Beautiful.
Sri Rama, the moss is like vermillion, Oh Beautiful.
Sri Rama, a female sculpture on every step, Oh Beautiful.
Sri Rama, a row of silvery fish, Oh Beautiful.
Sri Rama, a fully golden stepping stool, Oh Beautiful.
Sri Rama, having taken bath He stands on the stool, Oh Beautiful.

The poetic images of turmeric red waste, vermillion moss, female images on each step and the silvery fish are wonderful!

Another poem reveals the maiden's dilemma when she goes to fetch water at the well. It goes:

The well is deep, and the rope falls short.
How can water be fetched, from the top bank of the Bhammariya
well?
The bank of the well is full of mud;
While walking, the waist gets bent down,
On the top bank of the Bhammariya well.[10]

The frustrations and despair of the lovelorn maiden who goes out on the pretext of fetching water is expressed in the following song:

[9] This refers to a town in Gujarat called Dholka.
[10] The term *bhammariya* refers to a circular well which has a spiral stairway reaching down to the water. The term, however, also describes a type of garment worn by women.

The rope is forty arm lengths long,
Yet could not reach the water;
While waiting for the beloved one,
The day, after all is about to end

While she drops the pot into the water, she looks down into the well but thinks only of her beloved and sees his reflection on the water. The maiden does not let the pot sink into the water lest the reflected face of the lover be disturbed!

When the water level of a well is low, she is dejected but when it is full of water, she is overjoyed and then says:

In the farm of Bhavuba is Ratan Kuvo, a jewel of a well,
It can fill hundreds of water pots indeed.
Why then should I wait for the clouds to give me water?
I fill up the pots and so does my sister-in-law,
But look, at that very moment,
Her beloved, my brother comes to frolic!!

Thus, the stepwell, the pond, the stream, and the river figure prominently in folk literature and serve as a vehicle to express the feelings of love and longing, the sorrow of separation and thrill of reunion.

There are countless tales of love associated with the stepwells that have been transmitted orally from generation to generation. One of these is associated with a stepwell in the village of Vadthal in the Kheda district of Gujarat. It deals with the son of a landowner and his infatuation with the sculptural image in a stepwell of a beautiful *apsara*:

My beloved, O my beloved,
How deep is my love for you, my dearest.
Only when you cook will I then eat

Distraught at his behaviour, his mother says:

My dear Mubarak, where will this madness lead you?
The one you desire is no maiden but
A statue made of stone.

The young man responds:

Who says this is just a stone image?

To which she replies:

Everyone but you knows that it is made of stone

The son goes on to say:

You may think what you want, but the almighty has made her beautiful
and for me she is alive.

The mother entreats him to return home, but he refuses, insisting that he will go home only after he has eaten food prepared by his beloved. She tells him that the stepwell is the domain of the village women and they have not come there for the past 5 days because of his presence. Taken aback, he assures her that he will not go to the stepwell in the morning and evening hours at the time when the women come to fetch water, but insists that the remaining hours he will spend with his beloved.

Distraught by the young man's obsession, the family consults many doctors and soothsayers but all in vain. Finally, a shrewd doctor suggests breaking the image of the maiden. According to popular lore, only after the sculpture was destroyed did the young man recover from his insanity (Gaudani, 1980, p.151).

The popular and beloved songs of the Macchu Kantha region have found a permanent place in the folklore of Saurashtra. One such song narrates the story of a king who, when drunk, tries to harass a beautiful and respectable Baniya lady on the banks of the Macchu. The lady's response has the sting of the scorpion's poison making the king lose his pride and arrogance. The song goes thus:

A Baniya woman of Morbi goes to Macchu for water,
Behind her follows that Jivoji Thakor, to quench his horse's thirst.
Teases her, 'O Baniya woman, tell me the price of your water pot',
'Damn you, it is, do you hear, just your head for my water – pot!'

Another song describes the tragic outcome which ensues when a young woman defies and violates the norms of society:

> *Two sisters-in-law went to fetch water,*
> *At the farm of Sadguru indeed,*
> *Lowered the pots in to the water,*
> *Head rest strung on a branch of mango tree.*

> *There arrived a group of holy men then,*
> *They stopped at the farm of Sadguru,*
> *They played some games with dice,*
> *Did they and my husband's sister,*
> *Played some games of gambling they did.*
> *Ascetics lost the games,*
> *They lost and sister-in-law won indeed.*

The result of this thoughtless play with unknown strangers? Inevitable as it was, the sister-in-law narrated this reckless adventure at home. Alas:

> *Brother took out some poison,*
> *He put it in a golden bowl,*
> *Said now, 'drink it, O Sister of mine,*
> *You come from same mother as me.*
> *Drink this or else your sister-in-law will be blamed*

> *Looking here and there,*
> *Sister took the poison,*
> *Sat down with her sari wrapped on head,*
> *Alas! We put on her another colorful chundi for her.*

In this tale, the young woman is forced to commit suicide for her transgressions, namely gambling with strangers.

The stepwells and wells are analogous to and substitute for the beloved home of their fathers (*piyara*) where young girls can vent their heartfelt feelings and bare their souls. They have inspired folksongs, popular lore and dances. One such Gujarati song contains the yearning and longing of young women for their parental home where they had led a carefree life:

> *On the way to Vagad I feel thirsty.*
> *Build me a stepwell for I want to go to Vagad.*

The women's likes and dislikes, loves and anguish are reflected and linked to these buildings. They also serve as a metaphor for domestic relationships. One such folksong describes the return of a sister to her brother's home where she is disliked by her sister-in-law who ill-treats her in various ways. The sister-in-law asks her to live in the cattle shed and suggests she use cactus as a toothbrush and use lamb-dung as a mouth freshener!

> *May you go jumping over the empty wells*
> *And fall into a well full of water*
> *O my husband's sister!*

The song reveals the suppressed anger and frustration of the woman who responds to her oppression by wishing death on her sister-in-law. In a similar vein, a young woman complains to her husband about her condition and her resentment towards her in-laws. The real thorn in the woman's life is her husband's sister. She entreats her husband to remove the kitchen from the house, because the smoke of the fireplace renders her eyes red; her shoulders ache; and she wants her father-in-law to be sent out somewhere so that she has some privacy.

> *O My king! Please send the father-in-law somewhere, far*
> *To let him indulge in vain discussions.*
> *He makes me cover my face with the skirt end of my sari.*[11]
> *The thorn of berry plant pierced me, O My King!*
> *Send off your sister to her husband's house*
> *Along with her children.*

---

[11] This is a reference to the common practice of covering one's face as a sign of modesty, which is still prevalent among the orthodox.

Another folksong describes a beautiful woman who goes to the stepwell to fetch water where a thorn of love pierces her heart. She entreats her lover to come and remove her pain. It runs thus:

> *I had gone to a stepwell to fetch water,*
> *The neighbor woman accompanied me.*
> *Sent by my mother-in-law.*
> *And, a thorn of the Khra tree pierced me.*[12]

The young woman laments the fact that when she goes to fetch water, her mother-in-law sends someone to accompany her and keep a watch on her, thus limiting her freedom. The thorn which pierces her is really her in-laws.

Vadhiyar and Vagad regions in Gujarat are both arid and known for water shortages and droughts. The wells and stepwells there are deep and water in them scarce. It was said that water was obtained from these by beating on the drums. The *paniharis* who went to fetch water would lower their pots in the nearly empty well. When the pot filled up with water, the men would beat on their drums signalling the women to lift their water pots. In a region such as this, there was never any certainty of when a woman's pot would fill with water or when she would return home. Thus, the young women had to face the dual burden of scarcity of water as well as the ill treatment of their mothers-in-law. These poignant themes form the subject matter of the folklore of these regions. One such song goes:

> *O grandfather! Kindly do not give your daughters, like me,*
> *In marriage to someone in the Vagada region;*
> *The quarrelsome mother-in-law of Vagada is difficult to deal with.*
> *O grandfather! She makes me grind corn during the day, and spin*
> *during the night;*
> *Sends me to fetch water late at night prior to the break of dawn, O*
> *grandfather!*
>
> *O son's wife! Keep the knitted ring near your pillow,*

---

[12] This is from a well known folksong *Nanadala-Paronala*.

And rope near your feet.
And your seat you keep on the front verandah, O grandfather!
The pitcher sinks not, since the rope reaches not the water
My sun has arisen and set on the bank of the well.
O flying birds! Take my message to my grandfather
That your granddaughter has fallen into the well. O grandfather!

In another folksong from Mevas region, a young woman complains of a long wait at the stepwell and entreats her rich father-in-law to build a stepwell near their home:

Both the father-in-law and mother-in-law sit down to eat
Whilst the son's wife goes to fetch water from the stepwell.
Both the father-in-law and mother-in-law have finished their lunch
And yet their son's wife has not returned with the water.
Sixteen hundred maidens had gathered to fetch water
So, she was delayed in washing her hands and feet
Oh! Father-in-law! You are a great merchant;
Please get a stepwell dug just near the gate.

The sources of water have inspired various types of folksongs as, for instance, the following one. A newly married wife goes out to fetch water from a stepwell and is pricked by a thorn. No one could pull it out.

O My King!
We had gone to the stepwell to fetch water,
And, a thorn of a berry plant pierced me.
O My King! Please, summon the physician from Vadodara,
Let my foot be bandaged
The thorn of a berry plant pierced me.

Not all songs bemoan and criticise the in-laws. Occasionally, one gets a glimpse of tender feelings towards the in-laws. The song entitled 'Ekalo' describes the affectionate relationship between the mother-in-law and daughter-in-law:

> *My father-in-law is the King Ranamala*
> *My dear mother-in-law is the breeze from the sea.*

Another song reflects the happiness of the young woman and her fondness for her in-laws. It states:

> *Today in my dreams I saw the swaying hills,*
> *The gurgling river, I saw in my dreams, O my friend.*
> *The swaying hills are none other than my father-in-law,*
> *The gurgling river is my mother-in-law, O my friend.*

In other songs, the adversarial relationship between the two is also depicted:

> *This wily daughter-in-law has given a push,*
> *Drowning the mother-in-law, O my equal she-friend.*
> *The lady has sunk and her upper garment is floating,*
> *Lest she might turn back, O my equal she-friend.*

Thus, stepwells and wells inspired hundreds of folksongs which give vent to the frustrations and sorrows of the women. They frequently describe the bittersweet relationship between the mother-in-law and the daughter-in-law but also contain joyous accounts of their loves and their romantic fantasies. Here the women came to forge special bonds with other women and for support and friendship. These popular folksongs serve as a mirror reflecting the daily lives of the common people and enable us to glimpse their joys and sorrows, their hopes and disappointments. Through the medium of these songs, we can participate momentarily in the inner lives of these women. An understanding and appreciation of this folk literature enables us to lift the veil of anonymity and invisibility which surrounds these women, once again, making 'the invisible, visible'.

9

Art, Symbolism and the Iconography of Stepwells

The stepwells of Gujarat are unique architectural structures. They were built over a span of nearly 1,000 years during the reigns of both Hindu and Muslim rulers. The Muslim rulers of Gujarat were fortunate to have the skills and resources of the Hindu artisans and craftsmen, and often used the materials and stones from the earlier buildings for the construction of the stepwells. The latter, thus, took on a distinctive local form and reveal an exquisite blending of the Hindu and Muslim architectural style and aesthetics. Furthermore, since stepwells were primarily utilitarian structures and provided much needed water for the people, they escaped the fate of Hindu temples at the hands of Muslims conquerors.

WORSHIP OF EARTH AND MOTHER GODDESSES

Unlike Hindu temples, the stepwells became the focal point for folk religion and the worship of local goddesses and deities. Many of the stepwells were built under the patronage of women and frequented, by them. Thus, they represented women's space, and their iconography also tends to be unique. There seems to be a preponderance of the worship of earth and mother goddesses (*devis*) or village deities,

Saptamatrikas or the seven mothers, naga or serpent worship, Navagraha or nine planets; the moon and animals and birds, both mythical and real, including elephants, horses, monkeys, swans and peacocks.

These above-mentioned images abound in popular Hinduism and folk religion and are found prolifically in the carvings, sculptures and wall friezes of the stepwells. We will look at what is represented in the latter.

Shakti

Shakti is the creatrix of the whole universe. She is also the consort of Lord Shiva and in that form she is Uma or Parvati. In the Rani ni vav or Queen's stepwell at Patan, there are more than 15 images of Shakti in her many moods and facets. She is the divine mother; the *yogini* or ascetic practising austerity and penance; the benevolent mother; and Mahishasura Mardini, the powerful and ferocious warrior who fights the buffalo-headed demon and slays him, thereby saving the universe. Mahishasura Mardini, shown in the middle panel of Image 9.1, represents a warrior goddess who is powerful, aggressive and fierce. She has none of the characteristics of the gentle, benign and feminine Lakshmi, but instead is malevolent and a force to be reckoned with.

Local Goddesses

Of the many local mother goddesses or Shaktis worshipped and venerated in Gujarat and in stepwells are Limboji or Nimbdoji Mata (from the Limbdo or Nimb tree, which is regarded as the abode of Lord Vishnu and worshipped to ward off small pox); Amba (deity of the Jhala tribe); Ashapura (the deity who fulfils wishes of the Lad Vaniyas and Jadeja Rajputs); Asirmata worshipped by the Sonis; Bahucharaji; Bhutmata; Bhildi-mata of the Shervas, represented by a coconut; Chamunda worshipped by the Vaghelas and Chavdas; Devali mata of the Gamtas; Hinglaj mata of the Vegus and Darjis; Kalika, Mandavri of the Parmars; Meri mata of the Mangs; Randal

Image 9.1: Mahishasura Mardini slaying the buffalo-headed demon

of the Lohanas, Revalimata, Samudri, Sitala and Vaghesvari. Many of these local goddess are represented in stepwell art.

The Matrikas are worshipped on auspicious occasions when they are smeared with red lac, ghee, molasses and pieces of precious metal are attached to them (Enthoven and Jackson, 1989, p. 71).

Devi

Devi or the female deity is one of the most beloved figures of Hindu iconography. *Devi Mahatmya*[1] is the earliest known text which establishes the predominance and supremacy of the goddess. As the presiding deity of the village, the *devi* can be represented in the form of a rough, uncarved stone or tree. She ensures the fertility of the women and the crops, and the health and prosperity of the people.

The mother goddess is worshipped in myriad forms in stepwell art as Lakshmi, Parvati, Uma, Saraswati, Amba. Shikkotari, Sitala, Mahishasura Mardini, Suryani, Brahmani, Saptamatrikas and many others.

Saptamatrikas

In Vedic culture, the number seven had a powerful connotation; it was both sacred and auspicious. It signified unity, wholeness, completion and fulfilment (Harper, 1989, p. 27).

The Saptamatrikas or seven mothers are identified with the planets which influence the life of the child in the womb. One of the deities who presides over child birth is Randalmata or Rannadevi, the wife of the Sun (Enthoven and Jackson, 1989, p. 72). Saptamatrikas are the embodiment of feminine powers. They are the divine mothers who symbolise the Shakti aspect of the Brahmanical male gods. They represent life and death, sustenance and destruction and the concepts of fertility in humans, vegetation and water. As such, the Matrikas embody both the maternal and the warrior aspect of the female. As agents of fertility, they are benign, symbolising birth, rejuvenation and resurrection. Yet, they also carry weapons of war and become symbols of death. As Panikkar states, 'theologically, Saptamatrikas epitomize the creation, preservation, death and the final liberation of the soul, Mukti' (1997, p. 176).

---

[1] Composed in Sanskrit in circa 400–500 C.E., this text defines divinity as a female principle and narrates the victory of the goddess Durga over the demon, Mahishasura. It constitutes a segment of the Markandeya Purana.

OTHER HINDU DEITIES

The ancient text *Aparajitaprccha* describes the deities to be installed in the stepwells and the ponds. *Visvakarma Vastusastra* states that images of gods and ornamentation in the form of Kinnara should be made in the stepwell. Images of Varuna and other gods should also be placed in a water monument; Varuna is the god of the waters and is depicted riding on a sea monster or *makara*.

Uma–Mahesvara

Uma, the consort of Mahesvara, or Lord Shiva is frequently shown alongside him. According to the *Matsya Purana*, Shiva should be shown as having four or two arms, with matted hair on his head and three eyes. Like him, the goddess too should have curly locks and be seated on his left thigh. In her hand, she holds a mirror or a blue lotus.

Vishnu

Sculptures of Sesayin Vishnu are found in many of the stepwells. Vishnu is depicted reclining on a serpent in the primordial ocean. The serpent symbolises eternity. The many incarnations of Vishnu are also found in the art of the stepwells. Sesa represents the earth and the subterranean forces. Sculptures of Vishnu portray him with many arms holding the conch, *chakra* (discus), mace and the lotus.

Surya

The sculptural image of the sun god appears frequently in stepwell iconography. He is generally depicted holding two lotuses in his hands and riding a chariot drawn by seven horses.

Varaha

Varaha is an incarnation of Vishnu with a boar's head and a human body. He is depicted carrying a mace and other weapons in the right hand, and a conch and the goddess Earth or a lotus in the left (Image 9.2).

Image 9.2: Varaha with the Earth Goddess

According to mythology, Lord Vishnu as Varaha dived to the depths of the ocean to rescue Prithvi, the goddess Earth, who had been carried away by the demon. In Image 9.2, the sculpture in the centre depicts Varaha with Prithvi who he rescued from the cosmic ocean. She is shown tenderly stroking his snout. Under Varaha's foot is a lotus leaf that grows in water. Just below that is an entwined snake couple with human heads.

Kalki

Kalki is yet another reincarnation of Vishnu whose images are found in stepwells such as the Rani ni vav at Patan. Kalki is shown seated on a horse, carrying a sword, conch, disc and arrow.

Vamana

According to the Puranic texts, Brahma created a special deity, Vamadeva, whose mark was the *trishul* or trident. Also known as Vamana, the dwarf, he manifests the power of Shiva and embodies the principle of Kumara—the eternal youthful hero who is the symbol of life. There is a beautiful representation of Vamana in the Queen's Stepwell at Patan.

Dikpala

These protect the eight directions of the universe, the four cardinal directions and the four corners. These comprise Kubera in the north, Yama in the south, Varuna in the west and Indra in the east. The poets of the Rig Veda associated Indra with the clouds. He triumphs over Vrtra, the demon who is identified with the forces of darkness. Indra is shown riding his vehicle Airavata, the elephant (Savalia, 2000, p. 7).

Sarasvati

According to the *Matsya Purana*, the cosmic golden egg was spilt into two halves, male and female. The latter was referred to by many names—Sarasvati, Savitri, Gayatri, Brahmani, etc. Sarasvati, the consort of Brahma is associated with water and symbolises the sacred river. She is the patron of tanks, lakes and stepwells. She is also worshipped as the goddess of learning, knowledge and speech.

CELESTIAL FIGURES

Other sculptural images include that of Kshetrapala, the guardian of location; Navagraha or nine planets; the heavenly bodies Lakulisha; Sitala; Surasundari; and the *gandharva*s or celestial musicians.

Navagraha or Nine Planets

Hindus of all castes and classes worship the nine planets to secure blessings and ward off evil. These planets are believed to exert a positive or negative influence on the life of a human depending on the position of the planets at the time of one's birth.

Kichak

The Kichak is depicted in stepwell art as being short in stature, with a protruding large abdomen, scant clothing and an elongated face. These figures, who could be male or female, resemble dwarfs and appear as pillar brackets. In the Queen's stepwell in Patan, these images can be found in the ceilings and pillars. According to Savalia, these may indicate a Greek influence where they are called 'Amorini' (2000, p. 125). He goes on to suggest that most of the Kichaks from the Solanki age onwards are depicted in the *abhaya* (without fear) pose.

Kirtimukha

Another recurring feature in stepwell (and temple) sculptural art is Kirtimukha, a decorative form dating from antiquity and especially found in Chaulukya architecture. The *grasapatti* is a series of mouldings sculpted with grinning faces often in the form of Kirtimukha (victory face). The Kirtimukha generally show the full front face and tend to be highly stylised.

Apsaras

Representations of *apsara*s or celestial maidens abound in stepwell art. *Apsara* originally meant 'moving in the waters', indicating the fact that they were conceived of as water nymphs (Keith, 1925, p. 59). According to ancient Indian mythology, these beautiful *apsaras* preside over fertility along with the *gandharva*s (the celestial musicians), and those who desire children pray to them. These *apsaras* appear in the waters (both in rivers and clouds) as well as lightning and the stars. According to *Satapatha Brahmana*, they transform themselves into aquatic birds (ibid., pp. 94–95)

Gandharvas

Stepwell art also includes representations of the *gandharvas* or the celestial musicians who frequently appear alongside the *apsaras*. The *gandharvas* are depicted with animal-like legs, a human torso and a face which resembles a *garuda* or eagle.

OTHER NATURAL AND DIVINE ENTITIES

Amorous Couples

The depiction of amorous couples in stepwells and temples is common, especially from the Chaulukya age. These erotic figures of men and women are called *narathara* and generally occupy the space in basement moulding. It is very probable that these dancing, erotic figures follow the conventions prescribed in the *Kama Sutra* and *Natya Shastras*. They are found on both sides of the gods and goddesses.

Fish

Fish is a common motif and appears frequently in the stepwells. The *matsya* or fish signifies the emergence of life out of the primordial waters. *Matsya Purana* contains numerous explanations; one of these refers to the fish as symbolic of the cosmic 'egg', the cosmos being the egg of Brahma, the Creator. Within the golden egg produced by Brahma resides the life principle. In the Vedic cosmogony (*Satapatha Brahmana*), the waters existed as the primeval mother-principle. They desired to procreate and performed austerities. This produced heat from which was created the golden egg which floated on the water.

An exquisite representation of fish is found in the stepwell at Adalaj where a well cylinder contains a carving in stone depicting two fish in a playful stance.

Makara

Makara or the sea monster is the vehicle of the river goddesses Ganga and Yamuna. It appears in stepwells because of its association with water. It has a mouth like a crocodile while its tail resembles a fish.

Naga–Nagini (Serpent Prince and Princess)

There are frequent depictions of serpent kings and queens in the stepwells. These personify the terrestrial waters. According to Hindu mythology and folk tradition, the *Naga* and *Nagini*s inhabit the underwater paradise, dwelling in jewel-studded ornate palaces. They are the guardians of the riches of the deep sea—pearls, shells, corals—and protect the energies stored in earthly waters (Zimmer, 1946, p. 63).

Snakes are viewed as sacred in India's folk religions. In every village in Gujarat, there can be seen a shrine of Vasuki or Charmaria cobra. The image of the *naga* is worshipped on the bright fifth of the month of Sravana with offerings of milk, water, flowers, and durva grass. Charmaria, the serpent god, is offered *lapsi*, a dessert, on the second day of the bright half of Ashvin (Enthoven and Jackson, 1989, p. 63).

Elephants

It was believed that in primordial times, elephants had wings and consorted with the clouds. They possessed mystical powers to attract rain and could bestow long life, earthly happiness, abundance of crops and cattle and many offsprings. In Hindu mythology, Airavata, the divine elephant is the mount of Lord Indra, while Shrigaja is a rain cloud, the harbinger of rain. A pair of elephants also accompany the goddess Lakshmi. Because of their association with water, elephants appear frequently in stepwell art and in the panels and plinths. They are depicted with the goddess Lakshmi, or in a playful mood or fighting with the lion (See Image 9.3). One also finds elephants represented in rows, projecting from the base, as if supporting the building; such a base is called *gajapitha*.

Image 9.3: Elephants and lion at play

In the Rani ni vav, as well as at Adalaj, one can see carved animal motifs on the rows of mouldings on the plinth. Prominent among these are the row of horses (*asvathara*) and the elephants (*gajathara*). These are primarily for ornamental purposes and are a characteristic feature of Chaulukyan architecture. Craftsmen and artisans employed certain animal forms that could fit easily into certain spaces and repeated these forms to create a border, which was graceful and pleasing to the eye. This included Hathivela, Moravela and Phoolvela (elephant, peacock and flower vines) that were also found in the woven textiles.

Peacocks

Numerous depictions of the peacock can be found in stepwell art. In ancient India, the peacock gained its sanctity as the mount of Sarasvati, the goddess of learning. The peacock, however, is associated with the advent of rain and it is probably for this reason that it is found in water architecture. The left panel in Image 9.2 shows a peacock between the legs of the maiden who is attempting to thwart the snake.

Rivers

In Indian mythology and art, rivers are perceived as female divinities. They are depicted at the entrance to temples, as guardians and in niches, accompanied by wild geese, aquatic birds, lotuses and tortoises.

Trees

Kalpavriksha (the tree of life) and trees in stepwell art are symbols of fertility, abundance and long life. They represent the surviving remnants of nature worship, the origins of which date back to the earliest civilisation of the Indus Valley, 4,000 years ago.

Lotus

In the iconography of stepwells and temples, the lotus flower makes a frequent appearance (see Image 9.3 which shows a panel with stylised lotus motifs). In Hindu mythology, the goddess Padma or Lakshmi, the consort of Vishnu is depicted sitting on a lotus flower. 'According to the Hindu conception, waters are female; they are the maternal, procreative powers of the Absolute, and the cosmic lotus is their generative organ' (Zimmer, 1946, p. 90).

It is thus evident that the art and iconography of the stepwells differ from that of the Hindu temples. The patriarchal gods of Hinduism enshrined in the temples are less visible in the stepwells. Jain-Neubauer identified only three male deities from the Brahmanical Hindu pantheon in stepwell art, namely Vishnu, Ganesh and Surya (1981). What we see is a proliferation of local deities and the expression of popular or folk religion reflected in the depiction and worship of local goddesses, trees, serpents and vegetative deities. Stepwells, many of which were commissioned by wealthy female patrons and used by women, challenged the male dominant cults of Hinduism and the dominance of the Brahmin priesthood. They focused on immediate concerns centred around water, fertility and women.

It is tempting to put forward the hypothesis that, as patrons of stepwell architecture, women promoted not just religious but secular art. While Hindu deities, especially *devis*, are represented, the art and architecture of stepwells is still predominantly secular. Many stepwells contain motifs and representations of fish, *makara* or crocodile, tortoise and snakes which are not found elsewhere. These appear in stepwell art because they are aquatic creatures and symbolise water. In addition, stepwell art depicts *nayika*s, scenes of churning butter, women holding water pitchers or pouring water from pots, erotic scenes, scenes of fighting and acrobatic displays. At Adalaj and other stepwells, there are beautiful carvings in stone of vines or branches emanating from a vase resembling the *purnaghata* motif (or an auspicious vessel). The Patan wall with geometrical lattice work can also be found in Patola sari patterns and is yet another example of stepwell art which is secular in nature and intended to delight the senses and embody visual beauty.

10

Birds and Nature in the Stepwells of Gujarat[1]

The stepwells provided scope for the expression of artistic and aesthetic beauty. The beautiful carvings and images on the walls and pillars depict humans, divine beings, mythical creatures, animals, plants and myriad birds. With a few exceptions, they focus not on the male deities of classical Hinduism, but the female divinities, the local goddesses. Because water and women are pivotal in water architecture, the art too is inspired by these and transformed into women's art. The world of nature abounds here, specifically the depiction of birds and animals—both real and mythical—in stepwell art.

UNDERSTANDING OF THE COSMOS AND SIGNIFICANCE OF NATURE

An understanding and appreciation of stepwell art is not possible without some familiarity with the Hindu conception of the universe and the place assigned to nature in it. A unique and striking characteristic of the Indian worldview is the awareness and consciousness of the unity of life, the oneness of all creation and

[1] This is a revised version of the chapter 'Birds and Nature in the Stepwells of Gujarat, Western India', which appeared in Sonia Tidemann and Andrew Gosler (eds), *Ethno-Ornithology: Birds, Indigenous Peoples, Culture and Society*. Earthscan Publishing. London and Washington, D.C., 2010.

the resulting interrelatedness of all things—human, divine, animals, birds and plants. The man/nature relationship is not conceived in terms of the categories of 'dominance' and 'separation'. Consequently, the world of nature was perceived not as separate or 'apart' from human existence, but rather as an integral part of the cosmos. The law of *karma* binds all beings and nature in a web of unity. The fundamental principle underlying Hindu philosophy is that the *Brahman* or absolute reality is present in the soul or *atman* of each and every creature.

Thus from the beginning of Indian civilisation, nature was conceived as a vital force. The ancients viewed natural phenomena with awe and reverence. The earliest literary text, the Rig Veda, contains beautiful and tender descriptions of the beauty and splendours of nature. The forest dwellers or *Aranyaka*s, the holy men and sages strove to comprehend the meaning of life and unlock the cosmic mystery from their forest dwellings, where they lived alongside and in harmony with the birds and the beasts, the plants and the creepers, the sun, rain and the stars. 'Thus, it was that they could realize their own life by connecting it with the vaster life of nature around them. To them, their environment was not dead or vacuous, detached or insignificant, but the necessary context of their life' (Gangoly, 1963, p. 83).

THE PRINCIPLES OF *PRAKRITI* AND *PURUSHA*

In ancient Indian philosophical thought the universe was conceived in terms of two principles, *Prakriti* and *Purusha*—the former corresponds with the 'female' as well as undifferentiated nature, while *Purusha* was identified as 'male', as pure consciousness. These two principles from which the universe emanates were not binary opposites, but interdependent and co-existing. One cannot exist without the other, just as both male and female are essential to bring forth life. *Prakriti* or nature was perceived as the feminine principle, the creative and energising force behind the cosmos from which all things and beings in the universe are born. Thus, the Hindu ideology validated and strongly affirmed the 'feminine' and consequently accorded both 'women' and 'nature' a rightful and revered place in its cosmology. Nature, thus, occupies a central place in philosophical thought as well as in visual and other arts.

REPRESENTATION OF NATURE IN INDIAN ART

As Kramrisch aptly explains it, 'the relation of Indian art to nature is not conditioned by an optic impression of nature's forms but by the artist's inborn and deep love of nature' (1983, p. 128).

Nature in all its forms and glory, characterised by energy, vitality and a throbbing, pulsating force is represented in the stepwell art of India. The purpose of art, however, was never to merely imitate nature or to replicate it. Rather, it was meant to convey the spiritual essence that is inherent in the world of nature.

This personification of nature, the tendency to endow it with human qualities is a unique and distinctive aspect of Indian art. Water, the primordial substance from which all life emerges, is viewed as sacred. In the Sanskrit language, 'water' is equated with life itself. Rivers are personified as goddesses. Trees, plants, creepers and foliage are believed to possess tenderness and compassion, even more than humans. Plants, animals and birds mirror human emotions. The creeper depicted in Indian art as embracing and entwining the tree is equated with the lovelorn maiden embracing her beloved. The longing of the tree for the touch of a beautiful damsel called *dohada* is an oft-repeated theme in art and literature. It is said that the mere touch or kick from the feet of a lovely maiden can make the tree blossom and bear fruit. Thus in the motif of the *shalabhanjika*, an intimate association is established between the fertility and life-giving powers of the female and the fecundity and fertility of the trees. There is a positive association of women with sexuality; her life-giving powers are seen as sacred and auspicious.

Art, therefore, was not viewed merely as an aesthetic expression. It served a higher purpose, that of regulating the order of the universe.

BIRDS AND ANIMALS IN HINDU RELIGION AND LITERATURE

Birds in myriad forms occupy an important place in religious iconography. Birds occupy a prominent place in the mythological beliefs of ancient cultures and this was certainly true for India. They are seen as symbols of creation; their wings identify them with the skies and heaven. In the Rig Veda, Indra—the king of the gods who is also the god of rain—assumes the form of an eagle or rides on an eagle and kills the evil serpent Vrtra(Rig Veda I. 32).

There are numerous descriptions of birds in the religious and secular literature such as the Ramayana, Mahabharata and the Buddhist Jataka stories. The ascetics or holy men are referred to in the Ramayana as *rajahamsa* or *paramahamsa* because the swan or *hamsa* is endowed with the ability to separate good from evil. In the *Hamsajatakas*, the swan, which embodies wisdom, expounds the *dharma* or moral and ethical principles.

In Hindu cosmology divinities, male and female, are associated with an animal, bird or mythical creature which is their vehicle *vahana* or mount. Lord Shiva is always shown with the bull Nandi, Indra with the elephant Airavata, Brahma and Sarasvati with the peacock, Lakshmi with the elephant, Ganesha with the rat, and Vishnu with the boar. The animals are often depicted in human form and the boundary between human and animal is blurred or erased.

Many birds symbolise the individual soul. This concept goes back to the earliest religious text in India, the Rig Veda, which uses the metaphor of the bird caged in its body and soaring in the skies with the individual soul transcending earthly ties to become one with the Brahman, the infinite (Rig Veda of Hamsavati as narrated by Sudhi, 1988, p. 104). The birds soaring in the skies became the metaphor for spiritual liberation.

The Rig Veda mentions around 20 species of birds but it is probable that its anonymous authors may have been familiar with many more. Different birds are identified with certain qualities and virtues. The *Brahmini* duck became the symbol of fidelity; the eagle with its piercing eyes represented far sightedness and inner strength; the *chataka*, pied-crested cuckoo is said to drink only rain water no matter how thirsty and symbolised enduring love; the proud peacock was the harbinger of rain and the embodiment of joy and royalty; aquatic birds like storks, egrets, cranes and cormorants which breed during the monsoon season became associated with mating and sexuality.

Birds also symbolised carnal desires and emotions. Parrots were associated with courtesans who kept them as pets while peacocks were depicted in Sanskrit poetry as passionately amorous, their mating calls reminiscent of the yearning of the lovelorn for the beloved.

In classical Sanskrit literature, especially the drama and poetry of Kalidasa and Bilhana, there exists the accepted tradition of lovelorn heroines beseeching the birds for news of their beloved. Birds were viewed as messengers, which carried the message of the lover to the beloved.

Birds (and animals) were portrayed as friends and companions of humans. In literature they could think and speak like humans. They possessed wisdom and, like humans, they could be witty or heroic, cunning or noble, sacrificing or selfish, compassionate or cruel. The *Panchatantra* contains numerous depictions of animals.

The association of birds and animals with spirituality is a distinctive characteristic of the Hindu conception of the universe and, therefore, it is not surprising that this also occurs in stepwell art. Drawing from the fundamental beliefs of Hinduism, birds and animals are endowed with spiritual powers and attributes. They possess powers of transformation and symbolise spiritual development. It is because of this that in at least five of the ten incarnations of Vishnu, the creator god is represented in animal form or a composite of a half human, half animal form.

BIRDS IN INDIAN ART

Birds (and animals) have been from the earliest times a favourite subject of artists, sculptors and poets. Birds have figured prominently in Hindu and Buddhist art and literature, and are depicted in abundance and variety.

The earliest extant art in India comes from the Indus Valley civilisation. While the writing of the civilisation still remains undeciphered, thousands of steatite seals and other artifacts excavated since 1922 show evidence of birds in their art, specifically in their seals, terracotta toys and clay pottery. From Lothal in Gujarat (circa. 2300–1750 B.C.E), an important Harappan site, archaeologists unearthed a large earthenware jar painted with designs of birds with stylised trees and leaves in the background. The peacock is also represented in the pottery. Other excavations revealed miniature toys and whistles in the shape of birds.

This tradition of bird representation in art runs like a thread through thousands of years of Indian civilisation right to the present day. Birds are a dominant theme in sculpture as early as the Mauryan period (circa 321–185 B.C.E.). From the Buddhist stupas of Sanchi and Bharhut we have sensitive depictions of various birds like geese. Parrots and peacocks appear in the temple carvings and in votive tanks, evidence of the delight Indian artists took in depicting the many moods and myriad forms of the birds.

Ring stones found at Taxila, Mathura, Rupar, Varanasi and Kausambi contain nude female figures flanked by trees, birds, snakes, horses and lions both single and paired. Birds are also found in abundance in tribal and everyday art of India in the form of whistles, toys, toy carts, lamps, pipes and utilitarian objects as well as in ritual art. 'Bird-Mother' figurines abound in the art of Assam and West Bengal. These terracotta theriomorphic figures or *brata* dolls are associated with Bengali bird ancestors, such as duck mothers and other ancestral totem mothers (Raja Dinkar Kelkar Muesum, 1988).

There has always been a keen interest in birds and their habits in Indian culture. Emperors and members of the nobility (especially during the Mughal dynasty, circa 1526–1858 C.E.) maintained royal menageries and were intrepid observers of wild life. This deep interest in ornithology resulted in their commissioning artists to paint birds for their collections. Thus, Mughal miniatures paintings and Rajput art contain beautiful depictions of myriad birds. The latter depicts birds such as cranes and geese to highlight lovers' trysts on a dark night.

BIRDS AND ANIMALS IN THE ART OF STEPWELLS

The art of the stepwells is dynamic and awe inspiring. The images and carvings touch upon all the manifold facets of life and draw inspiration from the sacred universe of the deities but also from the fecundity and variety of nature. The art provides us with a glimpse into the entire panorama of life and as Sadani aptly states, 'Here art seems to mediate between the experience of the world and the experience of the transcendental' (1998, p. 53).

There are numerous depictions of birds in the stepwells of Gujarat. I have selected a few representative examples, most of which are from the Queen's stepwell or Rani ni vav from Patan built by Queen Udayamati in the eleventh century C.E.

This stepwell is the largest and most majestic of all the stepwells in Gujarat. It was commissioned by Queen Udayamati in 1063 C.E. but was completely inundated by the floodwaters of the river Sarasvati. In 1980s, the stepwell was excavated and restored after nearly nine centuries of oblivion. The stepwell is monumental in size and comprises seven storeys. More than 800 large sculptures decorate the seven terraces whose pillars, columns and niches are intricately carved with celestial maidens, Hindu divinities, mythological scenes and animals, trees and birds.

Serpents, Peacocks and Owls

There are numerous depictions of serpent kings and queens in stepwell art. The *Naga-Nagini*, serpent king and queen, personify the terrestrial waters. In Hindu mythology they inhabit the underwater world, dwell in jewel-studded ornate palaces and are the guardians of the riches of the deep sea—pearls, shells and corals (Zimmer, 1946, p. 63).

Snakes are viewed as sacred in the folk religions of India. Snakes and reptiles are associated with birds. According to prevailing beliefs, as a consequence of biological mutation, they acquired wings and became birds. Snake worship is quite prevalent in many parts of the country. In Gujarat, in virtually every village one can find a shrine of *Vasuki* or cobra. The image of the naga serpent is worshipped on the bright fifth of the month of Sravana with offerings of milk, water, flowers and durva grass (Enthoven and Jackson, 1989, p. 63).

In the Queen's stepwell at Patan, there are several exquisite depictions of the *naga kanya* or snake princess. Of these, the *naga kanya* with a fish bowl is one of the most striking and beautiful (see Image 9.2). To the left of Varaha is a maiden holding a fishbowl in her right hand. Clearly visible is a snake coiling around her left leg as if to reach the fishbowl. Her left hand is raised as if attempting to prevent the snake from advancing further in the familiar *tarjani* gesture suggesting a threatening stance. Of particular interest and noteworthy is the pedestal on the top which shows three owls in a sitting position. A peacock sits between her two legs with its gaze directed towards the snake.[2]

The three owls depicted on the panel above the snake princess may indicate night time since owls are associated with darkness and night. The owl is also associated with wisdom. Known to hide in the deep recesses of trees, it personifies supreme indifference to the world. According to one scholar, the bowl with the fish is a tantric depiction. According to Sadani's interpretation, the *matsya* or fish represents the ego while the serpent is the symbol of *kama* or passion. The Nagakanya with her raised hand in a gesture of restraining the snake may suggest the necessity to sublimate the ego and the passions that lead it astray. The peacock between the legs of the maiden is the natural enemy of the snake and represents non-attachment and control over passion (Sadani, 1998, p. 49).

According to the *Matsya Purana*, the peacock represents an antidote to the serpents' poison or demonic energy (Ibid., p. 258).

[2] I am indebted to Sadani for providing a detailed understanding and interpretation of some of these sculptural images discussed in the following pages.

The *matsya* and *kurma* or tortoise are represented in stepwell art because of their association with water. Interestingly enough, they are not depicted in Patan but at Adalaj, where there is a beautiful carving of two fish on the cylinder wall. This is also the case with the crocodile, another aquatic animal. The *makara* or crocodile appears in many Solanki period stepwells, including Adalaj.

The *garuda* or the eagle appears frequently in stepwell art, and is an important motif in religious literature as well as art. In Sanskrit, the term *gri* means to 'swallow', from which the word *garuda* is derived. It has been suggested that originally the sun was worshipped as a bird. The Rigvedic hymn (I.164, 46) describes the celestial bird as endowed with wings (Banerjea, 1956, p. 529). The eagle stands for the celestial bird. According to Zimmer, it symbolises the higher principle, 'the unbound spirit, freely roaming as a bird disentangled from the fetters of earth' (1946, p. 75).

It is said that the eagle is the natural enemy of serpents and destroys them. They stand for the fundamental opposition between the sun and the earth—the garuda identified with the former while the snake represents the earth and the dark forces of the underworld (Coormaraswamy, 1995, p. 331). Zimmer goes on to state that in Puri (Orissa) persons suffering from snakebites were taken to the temple where they encircled and embraced the *garuda* pillar. Thus, the magical powers of the eagle served to counter the poisonous effects of the snakebite.

In mythology, the garuda or the 'fair feathered one' Suparna or golden winged bird became the vehicle of Lord Vishnu. According to Zimmer, the motif of the heavenly bird was probably borrowed from ancient Mesopotamian art and suggests early contact between India and Mesopotamia. In both of these ancient civilisations, there existed the antagonism and battle between the heaven bird and the earth serpent. They are natural enemies—the former dwells in the sky and is identified with the sun, while the snakes living in the womb of the earth are the guardians of the underworld (Zimmer, 1946, p. 48).

According to Hindu mythology, Garuda is said to be the son of the sage Kashyapa and Vinata. He was born from an egg and has the body of a human, but the talons, wings and beak of an eagle. A rivalry between his mother and her sister Kadri, the mother of the snake, accounts for the animosity between Garuda and the snakes (Dallapiccola and Verghese, 2005, p. 82).

Geese or Gander

There are several beautiful representations of geese in stepwell art. The wild goose in mythology is associated with Brahma, the lord of creation. It represents in animal form the creative principle of the cosmos and is regarded as a symbol of absolute freedom attained through spirituality. In the 'Song of the Immortal Gander' revealed to sage Markandeya it states,

> Many forms do I assume. And when the sun and the moon have disappeared, I float and swim with slow movements on the boundless expanse of waters. I am the Gander. I am the lord. I bring forth the universe from my essence and I abide in the cycle of time that dissolves it (Zimmer, 1946, p. 47).

Zimmer goes on to explain the significance of gander and its association with a state of spiritual freedom. According to him, this is because of the effortlessness with which it moves from the earth to the skies above, the ease with which it navigates, from the terrestrial to the celestial realm and its ability to swim on the surface of the water and glide and soar into the sky. Holy men and ascetics who successfully emancipate themselves from the bondage and cycle of rebirth are equated with the gander. Like the homeless wanderer who has no ties to the material world, the gander is a symbol of unbound freedom.

Parrots

Many of the sculptural images in stepwell art depict parrots, which are favourite pets from time immemorial. According to texts like

Shilpa Prakasa, the heroine or beautiful maiden should be portrayed as smelling a lotus, garlanding herself, adorning herself with jewellery, adjusting her anklet or playing with a parrot.

Suka-Kanya or the damsel with a pet parrot is another exquisite panel in the stepwell at Patan (Image 10.1). It depicts a slim and graceful maiden standing between two ornamental pillars in what appears to be a classical dance position. Her raised right hand holds on

Image 10.1: Maiden with parrot

to a branch from which hang three mangoes and around it are foliage. Seated on her left arm is a parrot gazing at the maiden while the maiden too reciprocates with a fond look at her pet. The tenderness between the maiden and her pet parrot may symbolise the emotion of *vatsalya* or fond love towards a child (Sadani, 1998, p. 46).

Another impressive panel (Image 10.2) depicts a maiden standing between two beautifully carved pillars decorated with vines, creepers, foliage and possibly hanging fruit or mangoes. The sculptor shows

Image 10.2: Maiden and the swan

the maiden who has just come from her bath. She has draped her saree that clings to her still wet body revealing the contours of her sensuous form. She is shown squeezing the water from her wet hair, with droplets of water falling to the ground. Near her right leg, sitting on a pedestal is a swan which, mistaking the drops of water for pearls, is attempting to catch them. It is said that pearls are the favourite food of swans. The expression on the face of the maiden is serene and the artist has captured and conveyed not just the sensuality and seductiveness of the maiden, but also the world of nature and the harmonious coexistence of all forms of life—human, bird and plants.

The world of nature with birds and animals, as well as humans and divine figures carved on the walls and pillars of the stepwells still astonish us with their beauty, a reminder of a time and unique worldview in which birds and animals were our companions and equals in the spirit world, a world in which anything was possible, one in which mystical transformations took place between the human, animals and divine worlds.

11

Stepwells Today

These beautiful stepwells that represent the finest examples of water architecture ceased to be built after the establishment of British rule in India in the nineteenth century. The British administration viewed the stepwells with horror and disdain. They regarded the waters in these wells as unclean, unhygienic and a source of potentially hazardous infections. Regulations imposed by the British prohibited the use of the stepwells for drinking water. After nearly 1,000 years, the stepwells became obsolete and were replaced by taps, pumps and tube wells. Many were sealed and declared off limits while others crumbled to the ground, victims of neglect and disuse. In some cases, the stones of the ancient stepwell were carted away and used in the construction of new buildings. An even more bizarre use of a stepwell was by a local fire engine company, which utilised the waters of the well to extinguish fires. Those that survived are silent reminders of the past when they were alive with the sound of laughter and the voices of women who came here to fetch water, and others who spent a few hours here to rest and drink the cooling waters. The world of nature with birds and animals, as well as human and divine figures carved on the walls and pillars still astonish us with their beauty.

During my numerous visits to the stepwells in various parts of Gujarat, I was struck by the fact that some of these wells are once again being reclaimed, mostly by women. As Morna Livingston suggests, these have been transformed into 'embryonic shrines for the worship of local goddesses and female deities' (2002, p. 180). Women are once again claiming these structures as their unique space for the performance of rituals and worship centred on fertility, abundance, health and prosperity. Often a shrine to a local goddess which contains a sculptural representation of the goddess is constructed in or adjacent to the stepwell (Image 11.1).

Image 11.1: Mother Goddess riding a rooster

Image 11.1 is an example of a modern day representation of the goddess. Painted in bright colours, it depicts the local goddess riding a rooster, which is her vehicle. In her arms, she has several weapons—a trident, sword and possibly a book. Her right hand is suggestive of blessing her devotees.

In many of these newly constructed shrines for the local goddess, she is dressed in silk and satin with gold and tinsel, is often accompanied by her *vahan* (vehicle or mount), and holds weapons in her arms (see Images 11.1, 11.2 and 11.3).

Women from the surrounding neighbourhood come here to perform rituals of fertility and pray for the blessings of sons, health,

Image 11.2: Local goddess riding a tiger

Image 11.3: Modern day shrine of Devi

long life and prosperity. These images of the *devi*s attract the local women who converge here just as women did when they went to fetch water at the stepwells. The goddesses are offered marigold flowers, silk scarves, sweets and coconuts. Young girls come here to invoke the blessings of the goddess to ensure that they will find good husbands and happiness in marriage. Others bring offerings and pray for fertility and sons. In 2011 during a visit to one of the stepwells on the outskirts of Ahmedabad, I noticed a mound of clay pots in a corner of the stepwell discarded after the completion of rituals (see Image 11.4). This has once again become 'women's space' and serves the useful function of preserving these structures and protecting them from neglect and destruction.

Image 11.4: Discarded ritual clay pots

Image 11.5 shows the modern day structure built as an entrance to the Mata Bhavani temple in Asarva, Ahmedabad. The goddess with a trident is flanked by two lions. The lower panel depicts water pots. On two sides of the entrance are sculptures of elephants. This

Image 11.5: Mata Bhavani temple

ancient stepwell dedicated to the goddess has received a new lease of life. While not being used as a stepwell, it continues to attract worshippers.

Some stepwells—neglected, crumbling and dangerous—teem with all forms of life. Plants and creepers grow defiantly from the crevices of the stone structures, cooing pigeons and flying bats shatter the silence with the arrival of a stranger in their midst, parrots the colour of spring green share the space with snakes, squirrels, frogs, fish and turtles in the waters of the well. The birds and other carved creatures on the walls are being replaced by these new inhabitants of the stepwells.

For many years now, the stepwells had fallen into disuse, abandoned and neglected. Their stones were sometimes carted away to construct other new buildings, the images stolen and sold to art dealers. But, in the last few decades, they have once again been revived and revitalised, not just as a focal point for the worship of local goddesses but they are also being put to new uses—as the setting for concerts and classical music and dance festivals. In 2011, I had the opportunity to attend a water festival at Adalaj stepwell, which was organised to celebrate World Heritage Day. The magnificently lit stepwell glowed and shone in the night and reverberated with the sounds of the story telling of Manbhatt (a member of the traditional community of oral historians, folklorists and bards) and the rhythms of the electric guitar and tabla performed by a maestro. Nearly 1,000 people, old and young gathered at the stepwell on a cold, starry night to celebrate the glorious architectural heritage of Gujarat. Perhaps, listening to the music and the rhythms and melodies, the new generation of youth are rediscovering ancient buildings and, in the process, learning and reviving the legacy of their past. Queen Rudabai, who commissioned the Adalaj stepwell would have smiled for her prophecy found in an inscription there was coming true—'as long as the sun and moon shine, may there be joy and steadfastness.'

AFTERWORD

The scarcity of clean water and difficulty in obtaining it is still a primary concern for millions of women in India, especially in the rural areas. Traditionally, women were responsible for obtaining water for drinking and domestic use. With the demise of wells and stepwells and the explosion of the population in India, water has resurfaced as an urgent problem frequently leading to water wars and interregional conflicts. The failure of the government to adequately redress water shortage and meet the needs of the growing population has once again shifted the focus to finding alternative solutions and strategies in addition to the existing approaches. There has been, in recent years, a revival of traditional community-based water harvesting systems as a practical and affordable solution to meet the ever-present threat of drought and water shortages. Women and men are searching for innovative ways to solve the urgent need for water. Community-based initiatives undertaken in various regions of India have to date shown great promise. As an example, in Junagadh district, over two dozen villages have overcome the drinking water crises by launching a scheme that harvests rainwater. It is the women who have taken the initiative in this project—2,500 underground rainwater storage tanks have been built, which have successfully eliminated the need to walk 3 kilometres to fetch water.

Those regions which have experimented with rainwater harvesting and/or watershed development, show great potential in overcoming their problem of finding sufficient drinking water. This has also reinforced the belief that clean and sufficient water is a fundamental right of all humans. Perhaps the best way to safeguard it is to build upon the experience of village communities in water harvesting, conservation and management with the support of concerned individuals and the state.

We may need to once again listen to the wisdom expounded by the beloved poet of Gujarat, Dayaram Dalpatram (1896) who, more than a century ago, made numerous references to stepwells in his writings and stated:

> *Resettle the abandoned villages.*
> *Seek out the stepwells, wells, rivers, streams and*
> *Revive the old traditions.*
> *Make this your sacred dharma.*

Bibliography

Abbot, J.E. 1896. 'Bai Harir's Inscription at Ahmedabad, AD 1499', in *Epigraphia Indica: A collection of inscriptions supplementary to the Corpus Inscriptionum Indicarum of the Archaelogical Survey*, Vol. IV. Delhi: Motilal Banarsidass pp. 297–99.

Acharya, G.V. 1933–35. *Historical Inscriptions of Gujarat*, 3 Vols, Shree Forbes Gujarati Sabha Series, No. 15. Bombay.

Agni Puranam. A Prose English Translation by Manmatha Nath Dutt Shastri, Vol. 1, Chowkhamba Sanskrit Studies, 1967. Varanasi: Chowkhamba Sanskrit Series Office Studies.

Banerjea, J.N. 1956. *The Development of Hindu Iconography*. Calcutta: University of Calcutta.

Barot, K.C. 2006. 'Gujarat nu Apratima Vav Sthapatya', *Vidya: A Journal of the Gujarat University*. Vol. 1, No. 2, September, pp. 95–105.

Bayley, Edward Clive. 1886. 'Local Muhammadan Dynasties, Gujarat', in *The History of India as Told by its Own Historians*. London: W.H. Allen.

Bhatt, Krishnaram Ganapatram. 1914. *Vaghelavratant*, First Edition, Ahmadabad: Mehta, Hariprasad Pitambardas, pp. 191–93.

Bhattacharyya, B. (ed). 1950. *Aparajitapraccha*, Gaikwad Oriental Series, No. CXV. Baroda: Oriental Institute.

Bombay Presidency. 1896, Gazetteer of the Bombay Presidency, Vol. 1, Kathiawar. Bombay: Govt. Central Pres.

————. 1877–1904, *Gazetteer of the Bombay Presidency, Vol. 3, Kathiawar.* Bombay: Govt. Central Press.

Briggs, Henry G. 1849. *Cities of Gujarashtra, Their Topography and History.* Bombay: Times Press.

Burgess, James and Henry Cousens. 1902. *The Architectural Antiquities of Northern Gujarat, More Especially of the Districts Included in the Baroda State.* Reprint, 1975. Varanasi: Bhartiya Publishing House.

Burgess, James. 1874–75. *Report on the Antiquities of Kathiawad and Kachh.* Archaeological Survey of Western India, 1971.

————. 1896. *Architecture in Gujarat.*

Burton-Page, John. 1988. *Ahmedabad,* George Michell and Snehal Shah, eds. Bombay: Marg Publications.

Chaghatai, M.A. 1941–42. 'Muslim Monuments of Ahmedabad through their Inscriptions', *Bulletin of Deccan College Research Institute.* Vol. III, pp. 77–180.

Chaube, J. 1973. *History of the Gujarat Kingdom.* New Delhi: Munshilal Manoharlal.

Commissariat, M.S. 1938. *A History of Gujarat, Including a Survey of its Chief Architectural Monuments and Inscriptions,* 2 vols. Bombay and London.

Coomaraswamy, A. 1995. 'Transformations of Nature in Art', edited with an introduction by K. Vatsyayan. New Delhi: Indira Gandhi National Centre for the Arts and Sterling Publishers.

Cousens, H. 1926. *The Architectural Antiquities of Western India.* London: The India Society.

Dallapiccola, A. and A. Verghese. 2005. 'A Rare Narrative of Garuda at Thirukkurungudi', *South Asian Studies,* Vol. 21, pp. 69–71.

Dalpatram, Dayaram. 1896. *Kavya Bhaga 1.* Ahmedabad: Gujarat Vernacular Society.

Dehejia, Vidya. 1997. *Representing the Body: Gender Issues in Indian Art.* New Delhi: Kali for Women.

————.1999. *Devi: The Great Goddess: Female Divinity in South Asian Art,* Washington D.C.: Arthur M. Sackler Gallery, Smithsonian Institution.

Dhanky, Madhusudan and Harishankar Shastri. 1968–69. 'Davad ni Vav ane Gujarat nu Vapidhan', *Lekh Swadhyaya,* pp. 224–25.

Dosabhai, Edalji. 1986. *A History of Gujarat from the Earliest Period to the Present Time*. New Delhi: Asian Educational Services.

Enthoven, R.E. and A.M.T. Jackson. 1989. *Folklore of Gujarat*. Gurgaon: Vintage Books.

Enthoven, R.E and A.M.T Jackson. 1914. *Folklore Notes, Vol. 1*, Mazgaon, Bombay: British India Press.

————.1924. *Folklore of Gujarat*. Second Edition. Oxford: Clarendon Press.

Forbes, Alexander Kinloch. 1924. *Ras Mala, Vol. 1*. London: Oxford University Press: London.

Gangadharan, N. 1984. *Agni Puranam,* Part II, translated and annotated. Delhi: Motilal Banarsidass.

Gangoly, O. C. 1963. *Landscape in Indian Literature and Art*. Lucknow: University of Lucknow.

Gaudani, Harilal. 1968. 'Panihari and Panisherdo', *Lokgurjari*, Vol. 5, pp 52–56.

Gaudani, Harilal. 1980. 'Vadthal ni Vav', in *Mahagujarat na Shilpa ane Sthapatya*, Ahmedabad, pp. 150–54.

Goswami, Pranagiri. 2005. 'Kutch na Vav Kuva nu Sthapatya', *Lokgurjari*, Vol. 17, Gandhinagar: Gujarat Sahitya Academy pp. 192–98.

Harper, Katherine Anne. 1989. *The Iconography of the Sapatamatrikas: Seven Hindu Goddeses of Spritual Transformation*. Lewiston, N.Y. Edwin Mellen Press.

Havell, Ernest B. 1915. *The Ancient and Medieval Architecture of India: A Study of Indo-Aryan Civilization*. London: John Murray.

Hooja, Rima. (n.d.). 'Channeling Nature: Hydraulics, Traditional Knowledge Systems and Water Resource Management in India: A Historical Perspective'. http://www.infinityfoundation.com/mandala/t_pr/t_pr_hooja_book.htm

Hope, T. C. and James Furgusson. 1866. *Architecture at Ahmedabad: The Capital of Goozerat*. London.

Howard, R. W. 1967. 'Stepwells at Ahmedabad', *Architectural Review*, September, pp.227–230.

Hultzsch, E. 1969. 'Seventh Pillar—Edict', in *Corpus Inscriptionum Indicarum, Vol. 1: Inscriptions of Asoka*. Reprint. Oxford: Clarendon Press, p. 130.

Jadav, Joravarhsinh. 1997. 'Prachin Bharat na Jala Vihara and Jalakuunda', New Delhi: D. K. Print World, pp. 48–54.

Jain-Neubauer, Jutta. 1981. *The Stepwells of Gujarat in Art—Historical Perspective.* New Delhi: Abhinav Publications.

Jani, Shantilal. 1987. *Bharat na Nari Ratno,* Vol. 1 and 2. Rajkot: Pravin Prakashan.

Joshi, Umashankar. 1957. *Gujarati Lokasahitya Mala,* Vol. 1. Ahmedabad: Gujarat Rajya Lokasahitya Samiti.

Kadikar, Yashwant. 2000. 'Adalaj ni Vav', *Pathik,* October–December. pp. 54-59.

Keith, A.B. 1925. *Religion & Philosophy of the Veda & Upanisad, Harvard Oriental Series. Vol. 31.* Cambridge, Mass.: Harvard University Press.

Kumar, Savitri V. 1983. *The Pauranic Lore of Holy Water-Places: With Special Reference to Skanda Purana.* New Delhi: Munishiram Manoharlal.

Leyden, J. and W. Erskine, translated. 1921. *Memoirs of Zehir-ed-Din Muhammad Babur,* 3 vols. London: Oxford University Press.

Livingston, Morna. 2002. *Steps to Water: The Ancient Stepwells of India.* Princeton: Princeton Architectural Press.

———. 2003. 'Temples for Water: The Stepwells of Western India', *Natural History,* May.

MacMurdo, James. 1977. *The Peninsula of Gujarat in the Early Nineteenth Century,* Suresh Chandra Ghosh, ed. New Delhi: Sterling Publishers.

Majumdar, M.R. 1960. *Historical and Cultural Chronology of Gujarat.* Baroda: Maharaja Sayajirao University of Baroda.

Majumdar, M.R. 1966. *Cultural History of Gujarat.* New York: Humanities Press.

Mankodi, Kirit. 1991. *The Queen's Stepwell at Patan.* Project for Indian Cultural Studies Publications. Bombay: Franco-Indian Research.

Marshall, John. 1928. *Cambridge History of India,* Vol. 3. Cambridge: Cambridge University Press.

Masani, R. P. 1978. *Folklore of Wells, Being a Study of Water Worship in East and West.* Bombay: Norwood, Pa.: Norwood Editions.

Mehta, R.N. and Kanu Jani, 1961–62. 'Inscription in a Stepwell at Khadoli near Jhaghadia, District Broach', in *Bulletin of the Chunilal Gandhi Vidyabhavan,* pp. 31–34.

Mehta, Mridulabehn, H. 1973. 'Gujarat ni Kala Kushal Be Behno', *Pathik*, September–October, pp. 70–72.

Mehta, R.N. and Suresh Chandra Kantawala. 1962. 'Bhoj ni Vav no Sheelalekh', *Swadhyaya*, Vol. 16, no. 4, pp. 192–96.

Merutunga, Acharya, The Prabandha Cintamani or Wishing-Stone of Narratives, (History of Chaulukya Kings of Anhilvad, Gujarat, 746-934 C.E. Published ca. 1350 C.E.), Translated from Original Sanskrit by C.H. Tawney, Indian Book Gallery, Delhi, 1982.

Miller, B.S., ed. 1983. *Exploring India's Sacred Art: Selected Writings of Stella Kramrisch*. Philadelphia: University of Pennsylvania Press.

Moore, Charles. 1994. *Water and Architecture*. New York: Harry N. Abrams.

Nilkanth, R.M., ed. 1888. *Gazetteer of the Bombay Presidency, Vol. 2, Surat and Bharuch*. Bombay: Government Central Press.

Oza, Digant, ed. 2005. *Astitva Bodh: Jal Sanskruti*. Ahmedabad: Satyajit Trust.

Pandit, Shiv Prasad D. 1912 (new edition, 1982) *Bharat Na Stree Ratno, Vol. 2*. Bombay: Sastun Sahitya Vardhak Karyalaya.

Pandya, Mahesh Chandra. 1999. 'Uttar Gujarat ni Vavo: 942–1500', *Pathik, Dipotsav Ank*, November–December. pp. 87–100.

Panikkar, Shivaji K. 1997. 'Saptamatrika: Worship and Sculpture', *Perspectives in Indian Art and Archaeology*, No. 3.

Parihar, Subhash. 1999. 'Baolis of Punjab and Haryana', *Marg*, Vol. 52, No. 1, September, pp. 59–74.

Parikh, Rasiklal Chotalal and Hariprasad G. Shastri, ed. 2005. *Gujaratno Rajakiya ane Sanskrutik Itihas. Vol.4, Solanki Kala*. Ahmedabad: B.J. Vidya Bhawan.

Pathak, Ramanlal. 1997. *Gujarat na Jalashayo*. Baroda: M.S. University.

Possehl, Gregory. 2004. *The Indus Civilization: A Contemporary Perspective*. New Delhi: Vistaar Publications.

Raja Dinkar Kelkar Museum. 1988. *Birds and Animals in Indian Art and Crafts*. Poona: Raja Dinkar Kelkar Museum.

Rapoport Amos. 1969. *House Form and Culture*. Englewood Cliffs, NJ: Prentice Hall.

Rawal, Mukund. 1973. 'Gujarat na Vav-kuva', Pathik. July, pp. 53–63.

Rousselet, Louis. 1876. *India and its Native Provinces: Travels in*

Central India and the Presidencies of Bombay and Bengal. New York: Scribner.

Sadani, Jaikishandas. 1988. *Underground Shrine: Queen's Stepwell at Patan.* Ahmedabad: B.J. Institute of Learning and Research.

Sankalia, H.D. 1941. *The Archaeology of Gujarat.* Bombay: Natwarlal & Co.

Savalia, Ramjibhai Thakarshi. 1991. *Gujarat ni Hindu Deviyo nu Pratima Vidyan.* Ashutosh Savalia. Ahmedabad.

Savalia, R.T. 2000. 'Jal-Jalashayo ane Sanskruti', Chapter 6 in *Gujarat na Prachin Sarovaro, Talao ane Kundo.* Ahmedabad: University Grantha Nirman Board.

———. 2005. *Sanskriti and Kala.* Ahmedabad: Gujarat Sahitya Akademi.

Shastri, Hariprasad G. 1964. 'Gujarat ni Prachin Vavo', *Gujarat Dipotsavi,* Ank No. 2020, pp. 17–19.

———. 1991. *Shilalekho ane Tamrapatro: Vigato ane Viechan.* Ahmedabad: Gujarat Historical Society.

———. 2000. *Gujarat Under Maitrakas of Valabhi: History and Culture of Gujarat During the Maitraka Period, Circa 470–788 C.E.* Vadodara: Oriental Institute.

———. 2005. *Gujaratno Rajkiya ane Sanskrutik Itihas (Chaulukyas of Gujarat: History and Culture of Gujarat During the Chaulukya Period).* Ahmedabad: B. J. Institute.

Shelat, Bharati. 2005. 'Gujaratno Rajkiya ane Sanskrutik Itihas', in, Hariprasad G. Shastri, ed., *Solanki Kal,* Vol. 4: B.J. Institute.

———. 2007. *Gujarat na Sheela Lekho ane Sikkao.* Ahmedabad: Gujarat Research Society.

———. 2011. 'The Stepwell Inscriptions of Gujarat: A Cultural Heritage', *Journal of the Gujarat Research Society,* Vol. LVI, January–June, pp. 49–64.

Singh, Nagendra K. 2004. *Prabandha Kosa: Encyclopedic Dictionary of Sanskrit Language.* Mumbai: Forbes Gujarati Sabha.

Sivaramamurti, C. 1980. *Approach to Nature in Indian Art and Thought.* New Delhi: Kanak Publications.

Sudhi, P. 1988. *Symbols of Art, Religion and Philosophy.* New Delhi: Intellectual Publishing House.

Thévenot, Jean de. 1665. *Relation d'un voyage fait au Levant.* Paris: L. Billaine.

Tod, James. 1839. *Travels in Western India Embracing a Visit to the Scared Mounts of the Jain*. London: William H. Allen and Co.

Valand, Narottam. 2000. 'Gujarat ni Vavo', *Gujarat Dipotsavi, Department of Information, Government of Gujarat*, pp. 19–24.

Vaiya, Urmilabehn. *Gujarat Sanskriti Itihas ma Mahilao nu Pradan*. unpublished Masters Thesis, Gujarat Vidyapith, Ahmedabad.

Zimmer, Heinrich. 1946. *Myths and Symbols in Indian Art and Civilization*. Bollinger Series 6, Joseph Campbell, ed. New York: Pantheon Books.

About the Author and Photographer

PURNIMA MEHTA BHATT is Professor of History, Anthropology and Interdisciplinary Studies at Hood College in the USA, where she has taught since 1977. She completed her BA and MA in Indian history from Delhi University and has a PhD in African history. Purnima is the author of three books, *Scholar's Guide to Washington D.C.: African Studies* published by the Woodrow Wilson International Center for Scholars, Smithsonian Institution; *Shardaben Mehta: Una*

Mujer Exceptionale en al India de su Tiempo; and *Reminiscences: The Memoirs of Shardaben Mehta*. Her current research interests focus on the historical and contemporary roles of women in Asia and Africa; global perspectives on women, power and politics; women's leadership in peace movements; the impact of globalisation on women; and the African presence in India.

DANIEL DEL SOLAR (1940–2012) was a Latino media activist, documentatarian, videographer, photographer and poet. He completed his A.B. (Magna cum Laude) from Harvard University and went on to a varied career in public media and was a leader in innovative multicultural public broadcast. Many of his photographs have appeared in books, exhibits and on the internet. He was active in many Latin American social justice and solidarity movements.

Index

Abhineri, 17
Adadi, 97–98
Adalaj (Stepwell), 2, 23, 27, 29, 44, 49–50, 69–70, 83, 86, 116–117, 119, 128, 137–38
Adi-Kadi ni vav (Stepwell) 24
Agni Purana, 7, 11,16
Ahmedabad, 2, 22, 29, 40, 44, 49, 51, 54, 72, 136
Airavata, 113, 116, 123, 137
Amba, 17, 26, 30, 34, 108, 122–123
Ambamata ni vav (Stepwell), 58
Ambika, 29
    See also Goddess
Amrta, 6
Anhilwara Patan, 36
Animals, 2, 15, 38, 48, 53, 86, 108, 120–24, 126
Ankol, 20, 30, 38
Anupamadevi, 63
Aparajitaprccha, 12, 111
Apsaras, 6, 9, 29, 65, 75,89, 114

Aquatic animals, 29, 128
Arabic, 51, 53, 60, 70
Architecture, 1, 19, 21, 23, 27–30, 40, 51, 53, 72–73, 91, 114, 117–20
Art, 9, 25, 28, 36, 44, 64, 72, 78–80, 90, 107, 114, 117–22, 124–26, 128
Art Hindu, 44
    Chaulukya, 42, 72, 114–15
    Deccan, 65
    Islamic, 20, 43–44, 53–54, 70
    Mughal, 20, 43, 56, 125
Asapuri (Goddess), 54
Asapuri vav (Stepwell), 54
Ascetics, 8, 58, 96, 123, 136
Asarva, 40, 51, 53, 1
Ashapura, 108
Ashapuri, 24–25
Ashoka, 20
Ashvamedha Yagna, 16
asvathara, 86, 117
atman, 121

Baburnama, 20
Badula vav (Stepwell), 46, 60, 86
Bahucharaji, 108
Bai Harir Stepwell, 28, 44, 51
Bakula, 62
Balasamudra *kund*, 9
Baniya, 101
bauli, 17
    See also Vav, Baori, Stepwell
Betel nuts, 11–13, 34
Bhadra, 18
Bhadrai, 25
Bhadrakali (Goddess), 24, 27, 41
bhammariya, 99
Bhavani (Goddess), 20, 24, 30, 40, 136–37
Bhimdev I, 37, 62, 72
Bhinmal, 17
Bhoj ni vav (Stepwell), 48
Bhudevi (Goddess), 81
Bhuj, 57
Biographies, 64
Bird-Mother, 125
Birds, 9, 29, 58, 78, 120–26, 137
    and Nature, 120
    Aquatic, 9, 29, 115, 118, 124
Bisht, 19
Brahma, 3, 29, 33, 48, 74, 81, 86, 113, 123, 129
Brahman, 121, 123
Brahmani, 110, 113
Briggs, Henry, 22, 53, 70
Bundi, 17
Burgess, James, 21, 41

Chamunda (Goddess), 3, 54–55, 65, 82, 86, 108
Cambay (Khambhat), 72
Champabai, 55
Chamunda Mata ni vav (Stepwell), 55
Chandrabhagaji, 25
Chaulukya, 35, 36, 40, 42, 63, 72, 114, 115, 117
Coconuts, 11–13, 33, 136
Commissariat, M.S., 49, 73
Conservation, 19, 139
Cosmogony, 115

Dada Harir ni vav (Stepwell), 22, 51
Dalpatram, Dayaram, 139
Dasavatara, 42
Davad ni vav (Stepwell), 37
Dehejia, Vidya, 28
Derani ni vav (Stepwell), 45
Devanagari, 46, 49, 60
devis, 3, 33, 58, 65, 75, 81, 107, 119, 136
dhajas, 11, 13
Dhandusar, 45
Dhank, 36
dharma, 123, 139
Dhemi, 48, 60
Dholavira, 18–19
Dholka, 41, 46, 56, 62, 67–68, 99
Dholka ni vav (Stepwell), 46
Dhumdi, 48, 60
Dhyan Kaur, 30
Dhyi Hari, 23, 70
    See also Bai Harir
Dikpala, 113

Dirdhika, 18
Divorce, 61, 63
Dumral Bhagol ni vav (Stepwell), 38
Durga (Goddess), 29, 55, 65, 82, 110

Eagle, 123
Ekalo, 105
Elephants, 40, 51, 54, 86, 108, 116–17, 138
Enthoven, R.E., 7–8, 12, 34, 83–4, 109, 116, 127
European travelers
    Briggs, 22, 53, 70
    Jacob, le Grand, 22
    Rousselet, 22
    Tod, 21

Fergusson, James, 43, 69, 71
Fertility, 3, 8, 9, 30, 34, 78, 81, 94, 110, 114, 118, 122, 134, 136
Fish, 115
Folklore, 3, 9, 32, 64, 91, 94, 98, 101, 104
    See also Literature, Religion
Forbes 62, 66–68
Fuli vav (Stepwell), 58

Gandhak ki Baoli, 17,
gandharvas, 9, 12, 113–15
Ganesha, 43, 56, 79, 86, 123
Ganga vav (Stepwell), 38
Gangad ni vav (Stepwell), 38, 39
Ganges, 7, 49, 69, 85, 95–96
garba, 43, 91–92
garuda, 81, 115, 128–29

See also Eagle
Gaudani, Harilal, 36, 91, 96, 101
Geese, 54, 118, 125, 129
    See also Song of the Immortal Gander
Ghumli, 21, 22, 38, 45
Goddess (Devi): Earth, Local, 12, 84, 107, 112, 120
Gomtiji, 25
Goranji, 56
grasapatti, 87, 114
Gujarat, 1–2, 5, 8, 9, 11, 18–20, 27, 35, 51, 61, 72, 78, 91–93, 100, 107, 126, 133, 138–39

Halvad, 26, 47
Halvad ni vav (Stepwell), 47
hamsa (swan), 123
Hani vav (Stepwell), 45, 46
Hansu, 46, 60
Hanuman, 51
Harappan, 19, 125
Harper, Katherine, 83–84, 110
Hema, 48, 60
Hindu architecture, 40, 43
Horses, 54, 86, 98, 108, 117, 125

Iconography, 29, 42, 80, 107, 111, 118, 123
Indus Valley civilization, 6, 19, 33, 81, 118
    Dholavira, 19
    Harappa, 125
    Lothal, 125
    Mohenjodaro, 19
Inscriptions, 19, 24–25, 28, 39, 46, 51, 55, 60–64, 70

Isanpur, 58–59
Islamic architecture, 43, 54
istapurta, 28

Jacob, Grand Le, 22
Jain-Neubauer, Jutta, 1, 53, 119
jalachar, 8
Jaladevi, 12, 26, 46
Jansu, 46
Jaya, 18, 49
Jhala, 36, 47–48, 108
Jhilani, 35
Jhinjuwada ni vav (Stepwell),
    47
Jnana vav (Stepwell), 8
Junagadh collection, 46

Kalesvari ni Nal (Stepwell), 41
Kali (Goddess), 29, 48
Kalki, 79, 85, 112
Kalpavriksha, 54, 78, 118
Kalyande, 47, 60
Kama Sutra, 91, 115
Kankavati, 24, 42
karma, 121
Karnadev, 36, 40
Karnavati, 40
Karpurmanjari, 91
Kartikeya, 51
Kesarasar ni vav (Stepwell), 57
Kesarbai, 57
Khadoli, 57
Khanna, 30,
Khat-puja, 12
Kheda District, 38, 56, 68, 100
Kherali vav (Stepwell), 54
Kheralu, 94

Khodiyar Mata ni vav (Stepwell),
    59
Kichak, 114
Kilhana Devi, 46
Kinnara, 12, 111
kirtimukha, 38, 86–87, 114
Kramrisch, Stella, 122
Kshemankari Devi, 83
Kshetrapala, 12, 113
Kumardevi, 61
kumbha, 51
kund, 7–9, 16
kurma, 42, 128
kutas, 17

Laduba ni vav (Stepwell), 57
Lakha Fulani, 39, 97
Lakulisha, 12, 113
Lalteba, 18
Laws of Manu, 61
Limboji, 108
Lions, 54, 86, 125, 136
Literature, 30, 32, 87, 91, 106,
    122–24, 128
Livingston, Morna, 133
lok katha, 91
Lothal, 18–19, 125

Ma Ankol ni vav (Stepwell), 37
Macchu, 101
MacMurdo, James, 22
Madhav vav (Stepwell), 39
Mahi, 25
Mahmud Begada, 44, 47–53, 70
Maiden with a Scorpian, 79
makara, 12, 42, 111, 116, 119,
    128

Manasarovara, 96

Manbhatt, 138

mandapa, 17

Manikya Devi, 45

Manjusar, 36

Mankodi, Kirit, 1, 73, 75, 82

Mahishasura Mardini, 27, 38, 65, 82, 108–10

Marriage, 5, 31, 51, 61, 71, 98, 104, 136

Marshall, John, 20

Masani, 8, 10–12

Mata Bhavani ni vav (Stepwell), 20, 30, 40

Maternal love, 29, 87–88

    See also *vatsalya*

Matri Stepwell, 42

matsya, 42, 115, 127, 128

Matsya Purana, 7, 111, 113, 115, 127

Mayanalladevi, 41

Mehsana vav (Stepwell), 56

Merit, 2, 5, 6, 16, 27–28, 61

Merutunga, 61, 63, 64, 68

Mesopotamian art, 128

Minal Stepwell in Virpur, 41

Minalsar pond, 67

Mirat-i-Ahmadi, 40

Mithdi, 93–94

Modhera, 65, 73

Modheri Mata ni vav (Stepwell), 55

Mohenjodaro, 19

moksha, 6, 56,

Moore, Charles, 15

Motipura, 20, 36

Mughal, 35, 43, 56

Mughal dynasty, 20, 125

Muslim dynasties, 23

Naga Kanya, 127

Naga-Nagini, 116, 126

Nagar, 39, 46, 56, 95

Nanda, 18, 40, 74

Nanadala Paronala, 104

Narmada, 25

Narsinh, 85

Nature, 15, 23, 29, 44, 78, 97, 118–23, 132

Navagraha, 12, 29, 36, 84, 108, 113–14

nayika, 79, 89, 119

Non-Brahmanical, 29

Ossian (Stepwell), 17

Owls, 126–27

Padma Purana, 7, 87

panihari, 104

Parvati, 3, 65, 80, 82, 98, 108, 110

Parvati's penance, 82

Patan, 1, 10, 26, 36, 37, 45, 64, 68, 72, 74–76, 78, 81, 87, 90, 108, 113–14, 126, 130

Patan ni vav (Stepwell), 37

    See also Queen's Stepwell

Pathak, 8, 26, 27, 58

Patola, 78, 119

Patrons, 2, 19, 27–29, 36, 54, 64, 119

    Merchants, 5, 15, 26, 37, 44, 47, 55, 61, 105

    Mughals, 43–44, 56

Peacocks, 54, 108, 118, 123–27
Pilgrims, 15, 68
piyara, 31, 102
Polygamy, 62–63
Prabandha Cintamani, 61, 63–64, 73
Prakriti, 121
Prithvi, 112
Puranas, 6
    Agni, 7, 11, 16
    Bhagvata, 91
    Matsya, 7, 111, 113, 115, 127
Purusha, 121

Queen Hansoldevi, 38
Queen Minaldevi, 38, 40–43, 63, 65–68
Queen Rudadevi, 38
Queen's Stepwell, 1, 29, 37, 64, 72–79, 86, 87, 90, 108, 126

Rainadevi, 8
Rainwater harvesting, 139
Raja Virsimha, 49
Rajasthan, 11, 17, 20, 27, 30, 81, 92
Rajbai ni vav (Stepwell) 54
Rama, 69, 79, 98, 99
Randal vav (Stepwell), 27, 37, 48, 58, 72–73, 80, 83, 108, 112, 117, 126
Rani ni vav, 27, 37, 70, 80, 94, 97, 108, 126, 131, 126
    See also Queen's Stepwell
Ranibai, 48
Rannadevi, 84, 110,
Raskupika vav (Stepwell), 7

Ratno, 30
Resham, 23, 70
    See also Dada Harir
Rig Veda, 6, 10, 113, 121, 123
Rituals, 3, 5, 9, 11, 30, 33, 94, 134, 136
Roho ni vav, 55
Rousselet, Louis, 22
Royal hunting parties, 15, 21, 32
Rudabai (Queen), 27, 29, 49, 69, 138
    See also Adalaj Stepwell
Rukmini *kund*, 7

Sabarkantha, 9, 37, 42, 48
Sacrifice, 3, 16, 28, 39, 60, 94–95
Sadani, 1
Sajjabai, 55
Samari, 48, 60
Sanga, 26, 48
Sankalia, H. D., 40, 64
Sanskrit, 5, 11, 17, 28, 38, 45, 48, 49, 53, 54, 56, 59, 60, 69, 91, 122, 128
Sanskirt texts, 11, 20, 28
Saptamatrikas, 29, 36, 42, 82, 83, 108, 110
Sarangde, 47
Sarasvati, 48, 65, 73, 82, 85, 86, 113, 118, 123, 126
Saraswati, 72, 110
Sarovar, 7, 16, 73, 96, 98
Sasu-vahu ni vav (Stepwell), 41
sati, 47, 60, 62, 69
Sati ni vav (Stepwell), 59
Savalia, R. T., 5, 7, 8, 86, 113, 114
Selor stepwell, 8

Sesayin, 42, 111
Sevasi, 17
Shakti, 33, 70, 82, 108, 110
shalabhanjika, 122
Shastri, Hariprasad, 73
Shikottari Mata ni vav (Stepwell),
    24, 26, 30, 56
Shikottari, 24, 26, 30
Shilpa Shastra, 11, 21, 29, 33, 36,
    40, 68, 74, 75, 79, 83, 98, 108
Shiva, 3, 12, 29, 111, 123
Shivabavadi, 18
Siddharaja, 36, 38, 41, 63, 67–69
Sindhwai, 24
Singer Stepwell, 24, 60
Singer vav, 42, 83
Sita *kund*, 7
Sitala (Goddess), 3, 12, 24, 29, 34,
    42, 109
Sitala Mata ni vav, 57
Sodhi vav, 44
Solanki, 20, 36, 42, 62, 72, 114,
    128
Somnath Patan, 45, 46
Somparas, 11, 20
Song of the Immortal Gander, 129
Space, 1–3, 31–33, 92, 107, 115,
    134
Spirits, 6, 8–11, 13, 81
Status of Women, 60, 63
Stepwells, 1–37
    See also Vav
    Construction of, 6, 11, 17, 20,
        27, 36, 45, 48, 54, 61, 63,
        107
    Origins, 43, 118
    Rituals, 3, 30

Today, 3, 37, 45, 55, 133
Suda vav (Stepwell), 46
Sultan Begada, 23, 44, 48, 70
Sundari, 26
Surasundari, 12, 113
Surendranagar, 18, 26, 39, 59
Surya, 73, 83, 84, 111, 119
Suryani, 83, 110

Tapi, 25–26
Tashamadevi, 39
than, 59
Than vav (Stepwell), 9
thanak, 30
Thevenot, Captain, 22
Tintoui, 22
Tod, James, 21
Traders 5, 15
    See also Vanjaras
Troops, 15, 21, 32

Udayamati, 27, 37, 60, 64–66,
    72–73, 82, 90, 126
    See also Queen's Stepwell
Ugrasena ki Baoli (Stepwell), 17
Uma, 65, 82–83, 108, 110
Umreth vav (Stepwell), 41
Utvali Mata, 30,
Utvali Mata ni vav (Stepwell), 43

Vagad, 103–04
Vahanamati, 26
Vaikya ni vav (Stepwell), 38
Vaishya ni vav (Stepwell), 24
Vajeriyani vav (Stepwell), 8
Valhadé, 48
Vamana, 46, 79, 84, 113

Vamana Purana, 7
Vanjara ni Vav (Stepwell), 15
Vanjaras,15, 18, 54
vapi, 17, 56
vapika, 14, 17
Varaha, 51, 84, 112, 127
Varudi, 26,
Varuna, 6, 12, 111, 113
Vastusastra, 12, 111
vatsalya, 87, 88, 131
Vav (Stepwell), 7
Veena Vapi vav (Stepwell), 47
Vejaldevi, 54
Veshya ni vav (Stepwell), 55
Vijaya, 18
Virade, 47
Vishnu (God), 3, 29, 33, 36, 39,
    42, 48, 74–75, 79–81, 84–85,
    108, 111-112, 124, 128

Wadhavan, 95
Wankaner Palace, 59
Water Diviners, 11
    See also Rituals
Waters
    Conservation, 19, 139

Fertility, 9
Harvesting, 14, 138–39
Healing Powers, 6, 10
Purificatory Qualities, 6
Structures, 37, 7, 9, 14, 16–21,
    73, 98
Widow remarriage, 61
Woman's space, 107, 136
Women's clothing and ornaments,
    64
Women's patronage, 4, 28–29
Women
    Education of, 61
    Fertility, 3, 33, 34, 94, 110,
        122, 134
    Rituals, 3, 30, 33, 94, 134
    As Patrons, 2–3, 25, 36, 64,
        119
    Women's Art, 120

yakshinis, 81
Yamuna vav (Stepwell), 45
Yogini *kund*, 8
Zarmazaryan, 34
Zimmer, Heinrich, 25, 116, 118,
    126, 128